PETER N. CARROLL

Keeping Time

Memory, Nostalgia, and the Art of History

901
C 236

THE UNIVERSITY OF GEORGIA PRESS

Athens and London

84402346

©1990 by Peter N. Carroll
Published by the University of Georgia Press
Athens, Georgia 30602
All rights reserved

Designed by Kathi L. Dailey
Set in Mergenthaler Primer 54 and Fenice
Typeset by Tseng Information Systems, Inc.
Printed and bound by Thomson-Shore, Inc.
The paper in this book meets the guidelines for
permanence and durability of the Committee on
Production Guidelines for Book Longevity of the Council
on Library Resources.

Printed in the United States of America

94 93 92 91 90   5 4 3 2 1

Library of Congress Cataloging in Publication Data

Carroll, Peter N.
Keeping time: memory, nostalgia, and the art of history /
Peter N. Carroll.
p. cm.
ISBN 0-8203-1174-X (alk. paper)
1. History—Philosophy. 2. History—Miscellanea. I. Title.
D16.8.C34 1990
901—dc20   89-4905
CIP

British Library Cataloging in Publication Data available

Portions of chapter 12, "Living in Sin," originally appeared
in *California Magazine* (May 1985).

Title and part title illustrations by Fritz Hellmut Ehmcke
and associates first appeared in a catalog published by the
Klingspor Brothers Type Foundry in 1907. (*Graphic Trade
Symbols by German Designers,* Dover Publications,
Inc. 1974)

For a great teacher,
John J. McDermott,
formerly of Queens College,
now of Texas A&M,
who awakened a sleeping mind

Old houses were scaffolding once
        and workmen whistling

T. E. Hulme (1883–1917)

If you name a dog Time
and say to it
"Time, go back,"
what have you accomplished?

What have you accomplished
if you say to it
"Time, go forward,"

and it engages
the ratchets
of a new day?

William Dickey, *Brief Lives*

Contents

Preface

This is a work of nonfiction. The stories are true, but for reasons of privacy and discretion I have occasionally changed proper names, locations, or unimportant circumstances. The common thread of this book is the living history, the realization that all human beings inhabit not only a place but also a time. Although the chapters that follow focus on my own experience with history, the subject is not intended as a memoir—or, at least, not *just* a memoir—but rather as a case study of how history functions, how it impinges on contemporary life, and what its implications are for a citizen of the twentieth century.

For twenty-five years I have worked with a wide variety of historical studies: intellectual history and social history, colonial history and contemporary history, psychohistory and the history of the family, oral history and the history of film. What these diverse fields share is the effort to portray Time in human proportions, to make the infinite both manageable and understandable.

This book, by contrast, reverses that pattern. It serves instead to remind us that the particulars of ordinary life are indeed historical, that all humans, however obscure or important, exist in Time, and that each of us, like it or not, must live in history.

This work is also a plea for greater self-consciousness. History is not just a subject to be studied in schools, nor merely a topic to be manipulated by commercial advertisements, nor only an opportunity for political rhetoric, especially in election years. History constitutes a fundamental ingredient of our common cul-

ture, provides a sense of dynamic development, and so holds the
potential of better explaining the world and even changing it.

Many people have helped me along the way, but promises of ano-
nymity prevent me from mentioning all their names. Among them
was a friend from graduate school who named his newly adopted
mongrel after one of his professors and so took special pleasure
in wielding a rolled newspaper to housebreak the animal. Such
unembarrassed pragmatism adds another dimension to the poem
by William Dickey, whom I do want to thank by name for allowing
me to use it as an epigraph.

Closer to home, I've tried to rely on gentler methods of house-
keeping. Jeannette Ferrary, playing Alice to my Ralph, brought
plenty of insight, understanding, and love to this project. My children, Matthew and Natasha, remain at the center of the story. I
offer it to them as explanation.

I would also like to acknowledge the advice and encouragement
of several people who read early portions of this book, particularly
Michael Batinski, Rochelle Gatlin, Fred Hill, Frances Mayes, and
Jonathan Sharp. And Malcolm Call of the University of Georgia Press deserves a special thanks for his friendly criticism and
support.

Keeping Time

Gwendolyn, by Way of Introduction

We're flying to Paris, and the woman sitting next to me is sobbing softly into a wad of tissues. She is about forty, with straight, dark hair cut in a pixie style, a little plump. I avert my eyes and focus instead on the unusual name on her luggage tag. A celebrity, she is.

"I'll be all right," she promises, as the tears wash mascara down her cheeks and onto the blue-print peasant skirt that conceals, partially, her bulk. She is wearing many tasteful bracelets and rings, befitting her position and her fame on the airwaves. "I just can't deal with these separations," she adds.

Half an hour later, she is completely calm. Her voice is clear, professional. "I just can't handle goodbyes," she explains again, "ever since my husband left me." She is on the verge of total intimacy, one of those rapid outpourings of personality reserved for chance encounters in waiting rooms and airplanes. But it's a charter flight we're on, all seats reserved, round-trip, and I know I'll be seeing her once more, at the least. "I'm afraid of departures," she says, looking mournful.

"But this time you're the one leaving," I suggest.

"Isn't that the whole point?" she replies with a smile.

Thus baited, I pursue the conversation. I'm at the tail end of my sabbatical, having spent the past twelve months studying psychoanalysis. This year I've read virtually the complete works

of Sigmund Freud, and I'm learning to listen between the words.
But it's not exactly self-knowledge I've been seeking (not, at least,
professionally), but rather the application of psychological prin-
ciples to the study of history, which is my field of expertise. The
voices of the past—as I hope my airplane neighbor will now confirm—speak in a multitude of tongues.

I must pay attention to the words. And I must not alter their
intent by feeding her lines, putting words into her mouth. I choose
instead to become a recorder, thoroughly interested—fascinated,
really—but always slightly detached.

I do not expect to get drawn into the story. Besides, I've got
family problems of my own these days. This trip to Europe is also
a chance to see my little son. He was three when my wife and
I separated. Now he is four. Our distance disturbs my view of
myself. Am I just another father who has left home? Am I part of
the trend? Another statistic?

Do these concerns explain my enthusiasm for "the history of
the family"?

"Thanksgiving," the woman suddenly declares. "Married nineteen years, three kids, a big house in the suburbs. We were standing in the kitchen washing platters, the china. He told me he was
leaving."

"Just like that?"

"Just like that. I haven't seen him since."

He's been gone five years, and she can speak of him only as
an echo of some earlier self. It's not unfamiliar. We grow accustomed to losing people—not only through the epidemics of failed
love affairs and sorry marriages but: best chums from the first
grade who "moved"; anonymous checkout girls who quit to get
married or were fired; great-uncles and grandfathers, once relics
of the last century. They are intertwined with us—and then, one
day, they are not. Disappearances: they lure me deeper into the
past. I long to gather lost people; to resurrect their lives. Is this
personal compensation? Does it matter?

"It was a shotgun marriage," the woman announces with a
sudden brightness in her brown eyes.

"You were pregnant?" I blurt out, forgetting my professional
aloofness.

"Heavens, no! I was forced into my marriage to prevent any-thing like that from happening."

She'd been precocious. She started college at the age of seven-teen in 1948, and the place was crowded with ex-servicemen. She spent the summer going out with older men. And one afternoon her mother caught her necking on the couch. The fellow was twenty-three, an Army Air Corps veteran, then a college senior. "It was so innocent," she assures me. But her mother fell apart, terrified about what would happen next. "Is it so serious?" she wanted to know. The very next day her father interviewed the prospect. Within a month they were married.

"That was the way they kept me from getting into trouble. And that was the word they used. Trouble."

"Don't get into trouble in Paris," I quip.

The idea amuses her, at first. But the haunted look returns. "I don't know how I'm going to manage there," she says nervously. "I can't speak French. I don't know how I'm going to get around."

"I can be your translator," I volunteer, before I realize what I'm getting myself into.

"Would you really?" she replies instantly. "I wouldn't want to impose on your vacation."

I give her the name of the hotel Deux Continents on the rue Jacob where I'll be staying.

Two days later, at six in the morning, a sharp knock on the door drags me out of bed, and there on the landing she is, smiling sheepishly, with a handsome Arab teenager in tow. He, it seems, speaks no English; she, of course, no French. So far, it's been no problem, she explains in a hurried whisper. But now she wants to get rid of him, and he refuses to understand. So I take him aside and tell him about her husband, the marine, who will be arriving this morning from America. The boy nods rapidly and, without one word to the lady, rushes down four flights of stairs.

"What did you tell him?" she wants to know.

My own family reunion turns out to be uneventful. I bring my boy a small telescope, which, one morning, winds up in the kitchen garbage bag. I retrieve it without comment. I take him to playgrounds and parks, tie his shoelaces, buy sugarless gum and comics. We dine alone in neighborhood restaurants at an hour too early for my palate. I eat his leftovers. I read him *Huckleberry Finn*, transliterating the obscure vocabulary. In the end, I come to believe—need to believe—we can repair the damage between us. Meanwhile, my feelings toward his mother grow numb.

When I return to the airport the following week, I discover there will be an extra seat on the flight home because one of our group had gone swimming in Brittany and drowned. The husband accompanies the coffin through customs. Everyone else has the tanned, weary look of tourists on a budget. At the check-in counter my flight companion looks forlorn. There are dark patches beneath her eyes, which are red. When she spots me, she waves merrily. And after we're seated, she thanks me for the trouble at six in the morning.

"I'm glad it worked," I say.

"Oh," she answers, "but it didn't. We had a terrific time right through breakfast today."

"Is that why you woke me up at that awful hour?" I say, feigning anger.

"I am sorry about that," she says sadly.

As the plane races off the runway, she begins to sob. But I'm in no mood to commiserate. My brain tightens with anticipated culture shock and the realization that my year of freedom is over. I'll be bringing the fruits of research back to the campus, teaching a new course on the history of the family and another on "psychohistory." Having steeped myself in the unconscious, I'm eager to see how mine will work in the classroom. I'm intrigued by the relationship between ideas—how historians think—and the emotional factors that influence our lives. It isn't hard to imagine a convergence between one's personality and the kinds of scholarship that would be satisfying, if not pleasurable.

She has stopped crying. "I am sorry," she says. "I told you I wasn't any good at languages. I did need your help that morning. I wish I could speak better."

I assure her it's okay. Besides, she does speak well, at least in English. As a professional broadcaster she is skillful at forming perfect sentences in a perfect midwestern voice. Hers is the cadence of the nightly news, a distinctive inflection. It's ironic that she has, as she puts it, "trouble with languages." And at

the instant I realize she's used the word "trouble" twice before—
to apologize for waking me at that ungodly hour; to explain her
parents' fears of her sexuality—she provides, in the most matter-
of-fact way, the most intimate clue:

"I think I have trouble with languages because I was adopted."

"Oh, really?" I say in a tone of the cool shrink I fancy myself
becoming.

"I was always aware that there was something I didn't know
about me." Her "parents" told her she was adopted when she was
quite young "because some parents can't keep their children."
They said she was born in an orphanage in Chicago and that
they took her when she was two days old. "I was always frightened," she tells me. "I always sensed there was something no one
wanted to talk about."

She shows me an odd birthmark on the knuckle of her left
index finger. "I used to imagine I was an Indian princess and this
was the secret mark they gave me. I thought someday they would
come and take me back."

On Sunday afternoons she visited her mother's parents. While
the adults sat around the dining-room table, eating and talking,
she played alone, below. And then, abruptly, invariably, the conversation would shift to Yiddish, to something she was not supposed to understand, something mysterious about herself. In the
squall of language she was always afraid to inquire. "No one ever
told me—ever, ever," she says dramatically. "And I think that is
why I'm so obsessed, blocked, with languages."

"And with broadcasting?" I ask.

"My whole life is trying to understand that story," she admits.
"I felt trapped and had to work my way out."

So after she married and got pregnant, she went off to Chicago
to find out who she was. At the Cook County courthouse she told
the grandfatherly man that she needed her birth certificate in
order to get a passport. He said it was impossible; first, because
he wasn't allowed to give away sealed public records, and anyway it was down in the "dead vault." By law, adoption records
were sealed—still are in many states—to protect a child from the
stigma of illegitimacy.

"I was very pregnant then," she says, interrupting the story.

She describes a red wool maternity dress with plenty of fabric. "I was very warm and uncomfortable. And, you know, I was pretty young then and a lot more crazy than I am now, if that's possible. When he said it was in the 'dead vault,' I had a fit. I started to cry and scream and roll on the floor. I scared the hell out of that guy."

Scared him enough to go right down to the dead vault and come back with the sealed record of her birth registration. It held the dirty secret. On the last day of January 1931: Baby Girl (no name). Mother: Gwendolyn Rogers; father: Roy Rogers. Mother Cabrini Hospital.

That was it.

There was no Gwendolyn Rogers or Roy Rogers in any of the local phone books. No information available from Mother Cabrini, either. Then, she remembered something interesting: Her mother had a younger sister named Gwendolyn.

Her mother, caught cold by the question, confessed all that she knew.

Between drinks in plastic cups and other such airline interruptions, the story unfolds. "Minneapolis, Minnesota. January 1931," the woman says in a resigned tone. "Imagine the weather!" (We are both facing a long midwestern winter.) On mild days the temperature rises toward zero. The sky is blue as the Mediterranean; the sun sharp enough to melt the icicles that drip for a second and refreeze, forming marvelous crystalline lace that hangs from the snow-covered roofs.

Max, she tells me, was in his late forties, a small man (five feet six) with dark, curly hair, a big mustache, and a raised, flesh-colored mole above the corner of his mouth. He was born in Russia in the 1880s, fled the pogroms around 1910, and prospered in Minneapolis as a furrier. He had six children—one son, Sam, and five daughters—all with their father's beautiful wavy hair. (In this unfolding saga, little is ever said about Max's wife, though her role, my friend concedes, was probably of great importance. Thus is history selectively remembered and recorded.)

Of Max's daughters, his favorite was the youngest, Gwendolyn. She had clear blue eyes and a pretty smile. In photographs, my friend tells me, her curly hair overflowed a flapperish cloche hat. She was small, a little over five feet, but full-framed, with a large bust and round hips. She was not yet twenty on the morning Max took her to the Minneapolis railroad station.

She had passed through this station twice before within the year—when she went off to Hollywood to become a movie star and when she returned. She apparently was invited there by a distant cousin, a vaudeville actor who called himself Roy Rogers. They had met the previous winter backstage at the Minneapolis Orpheum, and he brought her to the cast party after the show. In April, when the snow was still stacked high against the curbs, she went west to see him again and discover what he could do to further her ambitions. "Well, you know what happened," says Gwendolyn's daughter. "He got her in trouble."

For months Max's wife brooded about this predicament, but not until Hanukkah, the festival of lights, did she confide in her husband. He was ashamed and angry. After all, Gwendolyn was the favorite. From his workshop lined with furs, he telephoned a distant relative in California, who explained that Mr. Rogers was now playing the Orpheum circuit in New York. The alternative no longer seemed so far-fetched as Hollywood. Max went home and told Gwendolyn to pack. They were going to New York City.

The train lumbered out of the station, groaned along the frozen track, and stopped fifteen minutes later in St. Paul. Gwendolyn wanted to get off and go home. Too late. The train moved east through the snow-covered dairy farms of Wisconsin, touched the Mississippi at La Crosse, rolled south toward Davenport, Rockford, Glenview, barely an hour from Union Station in Chicago, where Max planned to get a taxi to the other station to catch the Twentieth-Century Limited. But by then Gwendolyn, who had suffered from lower-back troubles since she was thirteen, twisted in pain. She could not endure another moment.

At Union Station Max was over his head. He hailed a cab and ordered it to a respectable nearby hotel. When they finally entered their room, Gwendolyn rushed for the bed. Max ran a hot tub and helped his daughter remove her dress, too stunned by her size to avert his eyes. He let her soak in the hot water, hoping the warmth would relax the muscles in her back. They would proceed the next day.

Before dawn, Gwendolyn was moaning again. Max had heard this sound six times before, and he knew what to do. He called the desk to order a taxi. Then he helped Gwendolyn dress and led her, half-crouched, down the hall, into the elevator, and through the lobby. Then to the nearest hospital. Max was only mildly surprised when they were greeted by a nun. In this case, he reasoned, it made no difference.

Nor, by the next day, did he see any point in continuing on to New York. He telephoned the news to his wife in Minneapolis. "We could keep her," he suggested. "Wait," she replied. They had another daughter, married, who might be interested. She told Max to call back in an hour.

She answered at the first ring. "Max," she said, "I forgot to ask. Is it a boy or a girl?" The reply delighted her. The married daughter would accept the child, but only if it were a girl. Two days later, the baby's aunt and uncle went to Chicago and took her from Mother Cabrini Hospital.

Gwendolyn was still not twenty. Her whole life lay before her. She appeared grateful to her father and her sister, but only mildly so. She insisted that they name the baby after a famous movie star.

My newfound friend, the broadcaster with the unusual first name, kicks the name tag on her flight bag with a stockinged toe.

After the plane lands, however, I do not see her long enough to discuss her autobiography again for several years. By then, I am living in California. I don't travel much any more. My son is old enough to fly alone, and he comes each Christmas and summer to restore his American identity. But one rainy day in mid-winter, my friend phones to say she is passing through on her way to southern California to visit her elderly aunt Gwendolyn, who is dying of cancer. I invite her to dinner and we chitchat about a multitude of subjects. Eventually she comes to the point. To my surprise, she tells me that no one outside her family has ever heard Gwendolyn's story, and that, in telling it to me aboard the airplane years before, she had felt unburdened for the first time in her life. Indeed, my interest had prompted her to undertake a fuller investigation, to uncover the missing pieces of her puzzle.

She had always referred to her aunt and uncle as her parents, even though she knew full well who her mother was. But she yearned to know more about her father. Who was this Roy Rogers and how could she find him?

His was a stage name, her parents had always asserted. And once, when my friend was little, they took her to the Minneapolis Orpheum to see him perform. But at the last minute her mother decided not to go backstage. My friend has no memory of the day, much less of any particular actor.

With this meager information, she traveled to New York City to visit the Actor's Equity office. There she confronted a shabbily dressed man who walked around with a cigar hanging from his mouth. He did not wish to be helpful, but impulsively he had rummaged through a three-by-five-card file. "You want Roy Rogers," he said gruffly. My friend said yes. "He died two years ago." Apparently, my friend's face changed drastically, for the man's attitude suddenly softened. "What was he to you?" he asked, almost sweetly.

"My father."

The cigar fell onto the desk.

Another year passed before my friend realized she could have obtained more information about Roy Rogers. But when she contacted Actor's Equity again, she learned that all the relevant material had been destroyed in a fire. She heard, however, that there might be surviving records in the theater archives of the Lincoln Center. Back she went to New York City.

The carton marked "Roy Rogers" was filled with newspaper clippings and press releases, but almost all of them related to the "other" Roy Rogers, the cowboy star. In the collection, though, was a legal settlement between the two actors with the same name. There was also a single clipping about the vaudeville performer from a Montreal newspaper that included a grainy newsprint photograph. He was a stand-up comedian. "He looked," says my friend, "like a fat, thick-lipped version of Milton Berle."

The cardboard box also contained a newspaper obituary, re-

vealing Roy Rogers's real name. It said, "He is survived by his
wife. He had no children." My friend was never able to locate his
widow.

Tomorrow, however, she is going to southern California to see
Aunt Gwendolyn.

"Will she help you?" I wonder.

"I'm afraid to ask."

"How can you afford not to?"

She didn't answer. In fact, I didn't hear anything from her for
about a year. Then, one afternoon, the phone rings. She is back
in town and, once again, on her way south to see Aunt Gwendolyn, whose cancer has reached a terminal phase. "She's not
altogether there any more, if she ever was," my friend remarks.
Gwendolyn had stuck to her Hollywood dreams, of sorts. After
returning to Minnesota, she worked as a secretary, then married a salesman of beauty-aid products, a dapper little man, and
moved with him to Beverly Hills. They never had any children.
He died ten years ago, and Gwendolyn has suffered from chronic,
excruciating backaches ever since.

Going through Gwendolyn's shelves, my friend discovered that
she had written a religious tract called *Harvest of Joy: God's Truth
His Message of Hope*. In the foreword Gwendolyn describes a life-
long ordeal with back pain, so intense that once she prayed to
God to take her away:

"Then, the MIRACLE happened that changed my life. I heard a
voice say, 'NOT UNTIL YOU KNOW MY BELOVED SON!'

"Seven distinct audible words ringing out loud and clear in the
darkness. 'NOT UNTIL YOU KNOW MY BELOVED SON!'"

When my friend confronted Gwendolyn with the knowledge
of her birth, the old woman had hardly reacted. All she would
talk about was Christian fundamentalism, to which she had converted many years before: NOT UNTIL YOU KNOW MY BELOVED
SON! But she did tell my friend, "If you were a boy I would have
kept you."

In her will Gwendolyn left my friend all her possessions and
property, including a modest home in southern California. The
person who lives in that house now is my friend's son, the baby

she was carrying when she visited the Cook County courthouse thirty years ago. My friend's other children are actors and entertainers.

"That's just what Gwendolyn, their grandmother, dreamed of becoming!" I observe in a carefully honed psychoanalytic triumph.

My friend smiles like a Cheshire cat: "It's just what their grandfather really was!"

I am moved by Gwendolyn's story—and yet unmoved. My reaction is not emotional. I see her instead as a "case study," an example of something outside herself and outside me. I do not get involved in such cases. I use them to make a point. The woman on the plane, Gwendolyn, Mr. Roy Rogers—they are testimony and proof of one of my history lessons.

"Most families have skeletons in their closets," my friend declared. "And in my family that was me."

Each of us bears a literal genealogy—the straight, dark hair of a missing father; his brown eyes; the lips. Each of us, I believe, also inherits, in a less visible way, a psychological genealogy, an emotional legacy passed from one generation to the next. Unchosen, often unwanted, this heritage provides continuity in time. It brings the individual lifetime, the private biography, into the streams of history.

My friend is not only Gwendolyn's daughter; she is also the result of an era. Her story involves the culture of Jewish immigrants just after the turn of the century. It touches on the mystique of Hollywood—ironically, another Jewish-American institution in the 1920s. It demonstrates the growing importance of modern urban values and mass transportation in what previously had been a provincial, rural society. It suggests the breakdown of the ethnic family in the face of melting-pot assimilationist pressures. And it hints at a restless, mobile way of life that has come to dominate the late twentieth century.

For what would Gwendolyn's story have been in any other age —in a time when there was no Hollywood, no railroads, no stage-struck teenagers in Minneapolis, Minnesota?

And my friend's lifetime—the story of the next generation—also speaks to the historical moment. She too is the product of time and place. So are we all. Even the most intimate, secret, forbidden wanderings of the heart exist inseparable from the reality outside ourselves. We mirror the opportunities and the limitations of our age.

This world where life and time converge—call it History—is the subject of what follows.

PART ONE

Beginning

Back East

ONE

Family Secrets

My mother is an unpretentious woman: diminutive, small-boned, easily accommodated. She has always felt deficient—unattractive, uneducated—although the reverse is true. Actually, she has fine features, moist gray-blue eyes, thick, straight hair, and a winsome dimple in her left cheek. She also possesses a long and tenacious memory. Her feelings of inadequacy, though unwarranted, express her humble background. She protests when I boast about her historical acumen. It sounds too stuffy and professional. She does not see that she has become, in her unassuming way, an expert on the history of the family. It was part of her responsibility as daughter and mother, woman's work. Of course, she never consulted a book on the subject, visited no archive; learned neither of coats of arms nor family trees. Instead, she relied exclusively on the oral tradition to acquire and preserve the historical record.

With a good ear for gossip and a passion for detail, she made herself the voice of authority about the family's past—why, for example, Grandpa and Grandma came to America; how they made their lives; what kind of politics they believed. This knowledge she leavened with intricate stories of explanation that she repeated and repeated and repeated. To ask my mother how she met my father—an event I know happened in 1933—invites a sojourn into all she knows about the family, from czarist Russia to the East End of London, and on to the streets of Harlem before it became black; a question about chicken pox evokes her sagas of childhood illness, miscarriages, and once (in a hurried whisper), abortion.

From such obsessions, legends are born:

Grandpa's mother died in childbirth; that's why he married an older woman. Grandpa never had a childhood; that's why he loved babies. Grandpa's father beat him; that's why he ran away from home. That's why he wouldn't become a tailor, like his father, preferring the itinerant life of a glazier who went from town to town to fix broken windows. That's why he was self-supporting as a teenager. That's how he came to know politics and to attend secret meetings.

The legend reaches a climax, well suited to a generation of native-born Americans: One night in 1905, the czar's cossacks surrounded a gathering of young men and began to fire into the crowd. At the sounds of shots, Grandpa fell to the ground, the dead and wounded and terrified piling on top of him. When the shooting stopped, he was covered with blood. To his amazement none of it was his. Later that night, the survivors retaliated by killing a cossack. But the next day the czar's shock troops ordered the community to turn over the murderer. The young men of the village met secretly again to draw straws. One was chosen. In the morning he was hanged in the town square. Grandpa decided to go to America. He was eighteen—and already married.

Grandma, so the legend goes, was ambitious. She came to America the year after Grandpa, in 1906, carrying their nine-month-old daughter. They could not afford an apartment at first, but Grandma found one anyway and raised the money for rent by scrubbing tenement hallways and hauling the garbage cans. Here she had her babies—two sons and another daughter, my mother. A coal stove heated the kitchen, but in the winter sheets of ice, formed by condensed steam, coated the walls. The boys slept in their parents' room, the girls in the kitchen on beds made by placing high-backed chairs together. They rented the second bedroom to a boarder named Mr. Jacobs, a formal old man who had immigrated from Germany during the Lincoln administration and who amused the children with his tales of old New York. Through the Roaring Twenties—Coolidge prosperity, the era of wonderful nonsense—that was how they lived.

Grandpa was a union man—proud to be a charter member of the glaziers' local. He spoke often of Labor Day parades and the funeral procession of working people who marched behind the victims of the Triangle Fire of 1911. Once, before World War I, he was out on strike for five months—an unbelievable hardship, given their poverty. And then the union lost. (Not until the CIO organized the building trades in the 1930s did the glaziers again have a union.) Grandpa was also a socialist and loyal to his class. Whenever anyone asked him who he would be voting for, he'd say he couldn't answer until he checked with his boss: Then he'd support the other fellow. Maybe that was why he never voted for a winning candidate before 1960, the first election held after the demise of the American Labor party. Yet Grandpa believed fervently in the electoral process. He was proud of his American citizenship and lorded it over Grandma, who couldn't pass the literacy test. It was his job to obtain and complete her annual alien registration papers, and he would use the occasion, each year, to threaten her with deportation. In her shame, she would want for words.

He was a short man—five and a half feet—with broad shoulders and a barrel chest. By the time I knew him, his hair was gray and mostly missing at the top; his thick mustache had become permanently yellow from nicotine. (He had smoked a pack of unfiltered cigarettes every day since around 1900.) Even then, he was working a ten-hour day. I never heard him complain about the risks of his job, though he had the scars and fractures to prove it: a broken leg, an arm, a cracked skull, smashed vertebrae—each caused by a different fall—as well as myriad gashes from the glass. Glass cuts, he explained, were clean. He didn't quit working until a series of dizzy spells added to the peril of climbing a scaffold. He was eighty.

The legend, as my mother shapes it, encompasses multitudes of names without faces—people born and dead years before I lived. Among them is my mother's older sister who, at the age of eighteen, went to bed one night with a headache and died before morning of a brain tumor. (My mother, who had slept next to her for years, has not had a sound night's sleep since.) As a young boy, I went once with Grandma to a cemetery in Brooklyn and watched in amazement as she pounded her fists against the earth in front of a white headstone, as if her peasant ignorance had caused the tumor to grow. Then she took me to another cemetery, also in Brooklyn, to show me the graves of her mother and father, my great-grandparents.

My mother remembers Grandma's mother, her grandmother, with three adjectives: tiny, sad, pious. Her husband, Grandma's father, lives in posterity with only one: filthy. Twice a year—he would tolerate no more—Grandpa would remove the old man's clothing, bathe and shave him, and give him a new outfit. The old clothes went into the garbage. These elderly people were brought to New York by their daughter because, as my mother says, "your grandma felt so lonely without them."

I visit my grandma in another loneliness. It is the winter of 1972—six and a half decades since she passed through the gates at Ellis Island. She and Grandpa are again living in one room in Brooklyn—in what is called an old people's "hotel." They are embarrassed about the surroundings, shamed to be counted among the weak and infirm. Grandpa, whose wit and vitality had depended entirely on the news of the day, has become sullen and angry. His red-plaid flannel shirt swims around his skeletal frame; his brown tortoiseshell bifocals droop from his soft hands. He is lost in a reminiscence he can no longer remember. When I lean down to kiss him, he blinks with the wonder of a child.

It's Grandma I've really come to see. She is eighty-nine. Her blue eyes are masked by cataracts and thick glasses; she doesn't hear very well. But her mind is quick, and she's pleased today to be the center of attention. My mother has brought her a bright-red dress. Grandma disappears with the box and returns in five minutes to show it off. The color contrasts with her fluffy white hair. It will impress the other residents. "Grandma," I say, "I want to ask you some questions." She is intrigued. She offers advice.

"They always told me to save for a rainy day," she says, leading me aside. "Then it rains every day."

There is no point in explaining to her the curiosity of the new social history—the interest in working-class women and the evolution of the American family—nor even to suggest (though such are my hopes) that a new magazine called *Ms* would surely want to add her to its list of "lost" women. It is sufficient for her that I am interested; she desires no more.

"What do you want to know?" she asks conspiratorily.

"Personal things. From when you were young," I add.

She takes my wrist and guides me down the corridor to her room. "I've got questions too," she warns.

In the small, dim room I can smell her cologne. "What questions?" I wonder.

"Tell me why you got divorced. What was the matter with her?"

I can see how much easier it is to ask than to answer. I suggest she go first. "Only don't rush me," she says.

She takes me back to the year 1903, to a delicacy shop in Minsk, where a dark-haired shop girl from the country acquired a taste for smoked fish and sweets as she dusted the shelves of glazed crockery and arranged the tins of chocolate. One day, while she swept the wooden sidewalk outside, she saw a young man with a black mustache carrying a pane of glass on his back. She offered him candy and, a little later, a kiss "not on the mouth." Soon they were talking about marriage. But her father, a blacksmith by trade (and, according to the legend, also a horse thief) insisted on meeting Grandpa's father, who in any case had to consent to the underage marriage. He arrived by train, took one look at Grandma, said "The boy never had a mother, he might as well have a wife," and then left on the next train. The young couple moved in with Grandma's parents. It was to this house that Grandpa returned, covered with blood, in 1905 and announced his intention to go to America.

Grandma shakes her head with pride. She knows that America is her most precious legacy, but she also wants me to appreciate its price, the ordeal of poverty and estrangement. When she landed on the lower East Side of Manhattan in 1906, she says,

Grandpa's wages were six dollars for a six-day week (and on Sunday, she adds, he went to the stable to feed the horse that pulled the glazier's wagon). With their infant daughter they lived in a back room in the apartment of Grandpa's aunt. There were no windows. The shop girl from Minsk was now the greenhorn, reduced to the family drudge: "dishes, laundry, floors from morning to night." Unlike Grandpa, she couldn't read or write. Nor was she interested in the socialist orators who attracted him to Union Square. She was left behind with strangers. When the baby developed croup, they sent her outside to sit on the stoop so the noise wouldn't disturb their sleep. Often she sat there through the night.

A few months after her arrival, Grandma discovered she was pregnant. She did not want this baby. She confided in Grandpa's aunt—who didn't want one either. The aunt knew a doctor, a Dr. Mandelbaum, who would surely help. Grandma told him the truth: "I don't have a place for the baby to live in. I can't afford another child." For ten dollars (nearly twice Grandpa's weekly wage), Mandelbaum prescribed pills, which Grandma took at bedtime for three nights. On the fourth day she returned to his office, where he sedated her and removed the fetus. It was painless, she assures me, easy, clean, good. Only later did she tell Grandpa why she spent the day in bed.

Grandma now fashioned her escape. She told Grandpa that they were leaving his aunt's apartment. When he objected, she traveled alone to the hinterlands—the east Bronx—and rented a fourth-floor cold-water walk-up. Here she would be free from relatives. But the move made her feel more isolated. She began to talk about going home to Minsk. Instead, Grandpa proposed bringing the family to her, and he devised a workingman's version of deficit spending to accomplish it. He made the down payment on a gold pocketwatch and chain—the largest investment he had made in his life—and immediately took the watch to a pawnbroker. With this money he made a down payment on the fare for Grandma's mother, father, and sister—people, it turned out, whom he learned to dislike. Grandma would not tell me why. Fortunately, a prewar boom in the New York building trades enabled Grandpa to meet the monthly payments for the tickets and the watch as well as pay the interest on the pawn. Eventually he would reclaim his treasured possession. Nothing gave him greater pleasure than to ping the gold lid softly against my nose as he explained how he had fooled the capitalists.

The arrival of Grandma's family coincided—it was an accident, she assures me—with the birth of a son. Four years later, she gave birth to my mother. She says the pregnancies were ordinary. Both children were born at home, attended, in one case, by a doctor (summoned frantically by Grandpa at the last minute) and, in the other, by a neighbor (when Grandpa wasn't fast enough). They were both breast-fed—which, says Grandma, kept her from having too many babies—and she weaned them by rubbing pepper on her breasts. There were now five people to feed.

Then, in 1913, she found she was pregnant again.

Soon after New Year's Day 1914, Grandma traveled to Harlem to consult Dr. Gordon, a general practitioner employed by the Workmen's Circle. He confirmed the pregnancy. Grandma asked directly for an abortion. Gordon refused. She persisted, pleaded, shrieked. Gordon changed his mind.

He would come to her apartment at nine the next morning. She was not to eat breakfast. She should purchase cotton and gauze for the bleeding. And she must tell no one.

That night Grandma explained her plans to Grandpa.

"If the baby is here," he objected, "it has to come."

"We have no money to support the children now," Grandma protested. "We can't give our children what they want. They live with bedbugs and cockroaches. Why bring more children into such a world?"

Grandpa relented. "Maybe you're right," he agreed, and went to bed. Rising early, he dressed the children, took them to stay with a neighbor, and left for work. Grandma nervously prepared: bathed, laid out the gauze, waited for the doorbell.

Gordon never came. Frantic and confused, she went to the corner drugstore and telephoned the doctor. "I'm not coming," he announced. "I can't take any chances." He explained that at eight in the morning Grandpa had roused him from bed and warned him against performing the abortion. "If you touch my wife," he threatened, "I'll have you arrested."

Grandma went home and waited for Grandpa. As he opened the door she attacked him—screaming, pleading, threatening to leave. He ignored her. It went on like that for several weeks, until it was too late to do anything. She swore never to forgive him, but now—sixty years later—it seems that she has. His own mother had died in childbirth, she tells me; he was afraid to tamper, afraid to lose her, too. Maybe, she confides, he was right.

On the eve of World War I Grandma delivered a second son. No one ever learned the fortuitous nature of his birth nor suspected anything unusual about his upbringing. But everyone in the family always knew that of all the children, it was this boy Grandpa favored most.

During the war, Grandpa worked overtime, but the peace of 1918 brought sporadic employment and lower wages. And Grandma, now thirty-four years old, realized she was pregnant again. This time she knew what to do, and she did not tell Grandpa. "I decided to have an abortion," she remembers, "because I could not feed my children. I would buy an orange and cut it into four parts, and I would have nothing for myself."

Through a neighbor, Grandma contacted a woman who agreed to help. The operation would cost forty dollars, however, an enormous sum. Grandma pawned the watch. And while the older children attended school, she took her four-year-old boy on the Third Avenue elevated train to an apartment in Manhattan. A half dozen women were already waiting their turns, but because her son was so restless Grandma went in first. The other patients amused the child.

Grandma lay down on a plain wooden table. "I will never forget that woman's face," she says, "for the pain she gave me. And then she told me that I lied to her because the baby was more than three months old." Grandma rested in another room mustering her energy for the journey home. Walking the stairs of the elevated, she felt a trickle of blood on her thighs, but she kept going. At home, she told the children she had a stomachache and went to bed.

She lay there for a week. Grandpa absorbed the news slowly.

He could never understand why a woman would risk her life not to have a child.

It was during this recuperation that Grandma first heard about birth control from one of her neighbors. "Her name was Goldy Trieber," she says emphatically, so I will get the name right. "Her husband was the tailor. She said, 'Your man has to take care of you.'" Goldy Trieber told Grandma about the withdrawal method: "It is better that he be half-satisfied than you become pregnant all the time."

Grandma told Grandpa. He called it "woman's talk." But considering the misery—and, perhaps, his guilt—he agreed to go along. From her thirty-fifth year, then, until Grandma reached menopause ten years later, that was the only method of intercourse they practiced.

"It was safer than the abortions," Grandma says earnestly, "and it was better than going without."

Grandma stands up. "Are you through?" Already embarrassed to know so much, I nod my head. She sits down. "Now you tell me." She wants to know about my divorce. I mumble something about "not getting along." She studies me with amusement: "Okay, don't tell me," she says. "Only live and be well."

As we leave the room, Grandma pauses in front of the full-length mirror. "You like this new dress?" she asks. "I have very nice children, but I'm not sorry I didn't have more. We couldn't afford them."

We return to the lobby, where Grandpa is staring blankly at a TV set broadcasting the hockey game of the week. In his more lucid moments he would describe the nighttime suspense of his escape from Russia, the bribed border patrol, gunshots in the forest, and then the hardships of steerage on the two-week voyage from Hamburg to New York.

"What's new," I ask him.

"What can be new?"

"What do you mean?" I ask again.

"We are old people."

"Well, what have you been doing?"

"What can we do? We are waiting."

TWO

The Family Song

xcept for their deaths, my father never spoke about his
parents. But one day, shortly after my conversation with
Grandma, he presented me with a brown soft-cover college
notebook that had a pole vaulter printed on the cover with the initials CCNY, his alma mater. The ruled pages were entirely blank,
however, until he flipped it over in my hands and began turning
from the back. Written with a black-ink fountain pen there was
definitely a story inside, but to me quite indecipherable, either
Hebrew or Yiddish with occasional block-lettered words in the
Russian alphabet.

"It's something my father wrote," he explained.

"What does it say?"

"I don't know."

The son of immigrants, my father preferred not to confront this
part of his past. Although my mother's parents spoke to him in
Yiddish, the Esperanto of Old World Jews, he always responded
in English and took a considerable pride in the results of those
long-ago high-school elocution lessons that eliminated all traces
of his ethnic heritage. He has struggled to be assimilated. He
even changed the family name.

"Why Carroll?" I asked once.

"It's a song," he replied, though later I would learn of more
complicated motives.

The identity problems of first-generation Americans are familiar: the unrelenting pedagogy of WASP schoolteachers; the urban gauntlet—Pollacks, Hebes, Micks, Dagos forever assailing each other for what they were not (the only baseball glove my father owned, he remembers, was stolen by a gang of blacks). In the tenements no help was possible with homework, with the memorization of, for example, "Old Ironsides." Shame was the first result. A friend of mine once overheard his father talking on the telephone in Polish; later, the old man steadfastly denied any knowledge of the language. In the same way, my own father never bothered to translate the notebook. Yet he gave it to me, the historian, his posterity. He also gave me his father's naturalization papers, an initialed gold ring that is too big even for my thumb, and a wooden-handled carpenter's saw. It is all that is left.

My mother can add only a few details. She hardly knew my father's family. She had seen his mother just once, on her deathbed in the hospital where the forty-nine-year-old woman was recuperating from gall bladder surgery. She seemed all right but then died the next day of a heart attack. My mother had met my father's father a couple of times: at his wife's funeral and, a few weeks later, just before his own. It was summertime, she recalls, and he was riding the subway to bring two fur coats to be put into storage. He apparently felt sick on the train and got off to find a toilet. At least that is where they found his body, lying on the damp concrete floor. The fur coats were gone.

My mother shows me a wedding photograph of the in-laws she never had. The woman is stout and round-faced like my father, and unsmiling; the man, dressed in a formal suit, appears rather dapper with a dark mustache and dark, wavy hair. "He was unfortunate," says my mother, tapping his face with her fingernail. "He was the kind of man that people took advantage of. He seemed," she searches for the word, ". . . meek."

My father is squinting over a broken flywheel on his workbench when I bring up the subject again. He resents the interruption. "My mother was a real bitch," he says ruefully.

With no further clues, I carried the little notebook across the continent to my home in California and asked a friend, who was

a member of Sha'ar Zahav, the homosexual congregation of San
Francisco, to attempt a translation. As is the case with many gay
men I know, he was estranged from his family, but perhaps for
that reason he was more than generous in embracing mine. It
took him several weeks to complete the task.

"I'm afraid," he announced as he delivered the handwritten
translation, "you're in for a disappointment."

"You mean it isn't Horatio Alger," I quipped.

"It is Horatio Alger—in reverse."

The story, which my grandfather entitled "From My Youth
Until Today," is tantalizingly skimpy. "I was born in a little village
in Russia," it opens, giving the place and family names, and adds,
"of parents who weren't rich." They had four children—two sons
and two daughters, none of whom are named—"and also a very
small house, the roof covered with straw, and inside was sand. On
the ground an oven to bake bread and a cookstove. Occasionally,"
he wrote, "we had a hen to lay eggs and a goat to milk which we
kept in the garden behind." Having read Turgenev and Chekhov
and Tolstoy, I begin to picture this life of utmost simplicity: the
bare floor, the smell of smoke, the scramble of children underfoot;
and I feel at once the stirrings of identification (so loathsome to
my father) with this peasant stock, the soul of Mother Russia. "In
summertime," the memoir continued, "my mother would plant a
few potatoes and a few beans and watermelon and green pickles.
And through the summer, we would pluck from the earth a little
food; for example, young potatoes with butter was a good meal
for the family."

My grandfather dwelled upon such delicacies not to evoke the
enchantment of a country childhood but instead to assert "it was
not always that lucky." The garden plot was only "as big as a small
prayer book. So there was not enough for winter. And we were
children with healthy appetites . . . and wanted to eat and there
would be nothing to cook. Then it wouldn't be so good."

These hardships—birthpangs of the American dream—were
suddenly mitigated by the arrival of a mysterious traveler from
a nearby village. My grandfather's father, it seems, was a gifted
singer whose "lovely voice," said his son, could be heard through-

out the village. He was well qualified to become the town's cantor
—the prayer singer of the synagogue—but someone else already
had the job. Nonetheless, the traveler was awed by the tremendous singing he heard. Here my grandfather interrupted the narrative—just as Grandma had insisted I record Goldy Trieber as
the woman who taught her about birth control—to tell the traveler's name: Zissel Talakanski from the village of Talakan. This
Talakanski immediately invited my great-grandfather to serve as
the cantor of his own synagogue on the coming holy days, promising to send a driver and wagon to pick him up.

"I was only eight years old," my grandfather wrote, and it is
from the eye of this child that the peculiar story is told. For the
driver turned out to be a gentile named Mitravchen, "big and
strong" with a big wagon whose bells "rang through the town"
and struck fear in the Jewish homes. "My father parted from the
whole family and sat in the wagon. The gentile with the big whip
gave a smack to the pair of horses and away he went. In our
house . . . our hearts were in terror." A few days later, Mitravchen
brought the singer home—along with fifteen rubles, a pouch of
snuff, and a large bottle of whiskey.

Now Mitravchen gave the little boy, my grandfather, a special treat. "I sat down in the wagon for a ride, or as they say in
America, for a 'free ride.' All my school friends were jealous of
me. I ride by all the shops and the bells ring . . . as all my friends
walk. . . ."

Thus began a tradition, harbinger of the Jewish New Year, that
lasted fifteen years—until my great-grandfather suddenly died in
his mid-forties. Mitravchen, the gentile-savior, came no more; the
free ride was over. My grandfather abandoned his studies, moved
to Kiev to become a carpenter, and carefully sent money home
to support his mother. It appears to have been a time of modest
contentment, if not prosperity. But then the gentiles again intervened. As my grandfather tells it in his memoirs, Czar Nicholas
issued a decree ordering that all Jews be converted, killed, or en-
slaved. "We were three days in an attic," my grandfather wrote.
"We came down to the street and saw great destruction, people
crippled and red blood in the streets and bedclothes with feathers

in the great city of Kiev and furniture broken and Jewish stores wrecked. A fear befell me."

Joining the Jewish exodus, my grandfather sailed for London —"a land of fog and darkness," he remembered. Through a marriage broker he met another exile—never mentioned by name in these pages—and married her, my grandmother. "A greenhorn must struggle," he observed, "that is already an old story, both with a new language and with earnings. And I tried my best. And the bread fell butter side down."

They decided to sail for America, where other relatives had preceded them, and settled in New York—first in Brooklyn, then in Harlem. The narrative describes the birth of three children— my uncle, my father, and my aunt—and records that "America satisfied me in every way." During World War I, my grandfather found good work in factories as far from his family as Detroit and West Virginia. But he was glad to go home when "the government didn't need me to travel any more."

"In 1919, I became a citizen," he recalled proudly; "I got a little help but not a lot."

There is only one more paragraph (except for a separate postscript) in these reminiscences. It shows that the memoir was written in the early 1930s. It also suggests just why my own father was so reluctant to examine the contents.

"And now I became a little older and weaker," wrote a man in his mid-forties. "If there were work, I could . . . make a few dollars. But unfortunately this depression has impoverished my customers, and in my trade they have started to use iron, brass, and copper instead of wood. But . . . we mustn't lose hope." He died in 1933.

Horatio Alger in reverse!

After he completed the narrative, my grandfather used the small CCNY notebook to collect various jokes, aphorisms, and poems—he may even have made them up—which indirectly reveal the state of his mind. Written during the dark days of the depression, the words reflect a mood of frustration, desperation, and shame. The writing is haunted by unhappy marriages ("My mother was a real bitch," my father had said) and by death.

For example:

> What's the difference between a tombstone and a wedding?
> The tombstone shows where one is buried; the wedding, two.
>
> Between an oven and a man about to be married?
> The oven burns with fire; the groom without fire.
>
> Between a bad debtor and a wife?
> A debtor says he'll pay you some day; a wife pays you immediately.

In his rhymes and adages my grandfather was also preoccupied by success and his inability to achieve it:

> Many great men are discovered first by the writing on their tombstone.
> A great man is like an actor. He is applauded only after he has left the stage.
> A politician always promises; a boss always fires.
>
> *Father:* My child, rising early is very good. There was a man who got up early every day and found a purse with gold.
> *Son:* Yes, but he who lost the purse got up even earlier.

The last entry in the book offers not even a wisp of his wit: "On three things the world stands—on Torah, on work, on mercy. But in America all three are missing. That's why life is ruined here."

He died, as I said, in a subway toilet.

His ambitions passed to his American-born children. My father also wanted desperately to succeed, and he showed remarkable potential as a boy, skipping grades every other year and finishing high school at the age of fourteen. By then, he was also an accomplished pianist. But the year was 1929, and before long, hard times were pinching at his dreams. In the daytime he attended CCNY (where my grandfather got his notebook); with his father unemployed, he worked at night playing the piano in nightclubs and dance halls around Manhattan. I have a photograph of the fifteen-year-old musician, dressed like a juvenile Oscar Levant in a bow tie and dark, round-framed glasses, sitting behind a keyboard with his homework propped on the piano. Then, in rapid order, his parents died, he married my mother, and they had a baby, my sister. He was not yet twenty.

Like so many others of his generation, my father was thwarted by the depression, by the sheer difficulty of earning wages to pay for his food. He admitted to me that he once sneaked into a neighbor's apartment and stole a pot of soup bubbling on the stove. "I was hungry," he said. Eventually he found jobs as an arranger and copyist for musical broadcasting companies, transcribing compositions by hand, and he continued to play club dates, teach piano, and write songs. He wanted to be a composer or, at the least, a conductor. But the firms that employed him offered no outlets for his originality.

Historians who have studied the psychology of the Great Depression emphasize the self-destructiveness caused by unemployment and poverty, the fact that Americans blamed themselves rather than the capitalist system for their failures. That is not true of my father. He was not a good businessman, nor even a good worker. When frustrated by one employer, he actually quit his job, depression or not, and later launched his own recording company, which became moderately successful only after he had left it. Yet he attributed his problems to the social order that surrounded him. Just as his own father felt a child's pride in riding around the village in Mitravchen's wagon, my father sought to overcome a pervasive anti-Semitism that kept him apart and down. "Carroll" was not only a song but an assimilationist cry for acceptability. In the end, the new name did not help his career (nor hurt it either), but it provided the next generation, mine, with an ethnic cloak. I inherited different problems; I spent my childhood explaining that Carroll was not a girl's name.

My father also understood the language of the class struggle. His interest in intellectual debate and his flair for the arts pushed him toward the political left. He saw his impoverishment as the result of capitalist greed. He thought patriotism was completely compatible with the coming of a socialist state. He joined the Communist party and, in small ways, participated in the radical movement. He played the piano at fund-raisers to support Americans fighting in the Spanish civil war; he opposed racial discrimination in neighborhood housing. Recently, my mother mentioned that their "secret" name in the CP was Carroll.

These personal responses to the depression—the desire for assimilation, joining the communist movement—proved less enduring than other psychological legacies. Having survived hard times (and afterward the war), my father never surrendered his belief that success in America was possible. If he had been unfortunate in his upbringing, in the economic realities of the 1930s, then like his own father he would project his ambitions onto his children. Of all the many pedagogical certitudes he espoused, none was more often spoken than the demand that I *not* work my way through college. I would enjoy the luxury he had lost, and he even wrote his will in such a way as to insure my academic future. (Later, when I won a full fellowship to graduate school, his pride was mixed with an abrupt feeling of anachronism).

But if the thwarted hopes of the depression generation were affixed to the children of my generation, there was also an implicit, subliminal message that warned of the dangers of success. While encouraging us to embrace the American dream, my father's generation also transmitted the idea—certainly the feeling—that adulthood was a time of weighty responsibility, of deferred desire and gratification; in short, a trap. Marriage, career, kids—that was the end of the line. Here, I suspect, lay the psychological roots of the 1960s counterculture, the rejection of responsibility and adulthood and the affirmation "don't trust anyone over thirty." Growing up was giving up. Yet my father was constantly rebelling against the notion of a settled career. As soon as I did win that fellowship, he moved quickly toward early retirement, glad to abandon the routines of the normal workday, the obligation to wear a white shirt and a tie, even to wash his hands. In the end, my father knew how to quit a job, and his example, years later, emboldened me to make that a family tradition too.

THREE

The Best Years

Alex Haley calls it "stardust," the dialogue between grandparents and grandchildren. I would lie beneath the kitchen table on the linoleum floor and listen. Each story concerned a tapestry of characters that lived just beyond the threshold of memory. That was the magic: an immediacy always outside my reach. This past was too close to be learned from books, and too far ever to be mine. I envied their time.

Four decades later, Grandpa and Grandma are dead, my uncles and aunts are dead, my father is dead, and I try to resurrect moments when all I could do was listen. My mother alone survives, and she is skeptical about my interest. Her memories disturb her, evoke old anxieties and new ones. I know that my grandparents were there so much because my father was not. But when I inquire about the early years of her marriage, she replies, "Time moves faster now than when I was younger." She will reveal the past, I surmise, only by indirection.

So I ask my mother to talk about food. It has always been her domain, the heritage of women, daily responsibilities that add up, meal upon meal, into a tradition. What will I learn from her food? She expresses no interest, however, beyond necessity. She reminds me, as if I could ever forget, that usually, which is to say every day, she made meat, a green vegetable, a "starch" (she means potato), and dessert.

She pauses for my response: I could wax nostalgic about Mom's apple pie, orange cookies with colored sprinkles, or a fresh lemon meringue—these she makes now for my daughter—but the fact is, I remember best the Del Monte fruit cocktail, one maraschino cherry per serving because two meant my sister would have a fit, or sliced peaches in syrup. Her culinary style was frugal: The portions were small, and she distrusted sauces, herbs, spices, whatever could not be seen, whatever added surprise. Old photographs reveal an extraordinarily skinny girl; she weighed eighty-eight pounds when she was married. Was she anorexic?

"It was depression," she says; "we had to make do."

"Mom," I say, trying to be funny; "you mean *depressing.*"

She smiles. "You're just like your father. He was the same way. . . ."

Her stock answer suddenly flashes into my memory with the force of Proust's madeleine. To my delight, I can finish the sentence myself: ". . . until he went into the army. Then he appreciated good home cooking." Through my childhood and adolescence, that was the reply to all my complaints about her cooking, and even then I thought there was something slightly ridiculous about taking satisfaction in outcooking the army. But now, with a better ear for nuance, I hear something else in the old refrain about how my father never appreciated her cooking. It is just what I'm after.

"Until he went into the army": a phrase endlessly repeated. How traumatic the war must have been, the point that divided their lives into a before and an after. It was the one time my father left home to see the world; it was the one time (until he died) that my mother was left behind. It was the one time—the single opportunity—when he might not have come back at all. But, of course, he did and once he did, their ambitions (what they had dreamed about "until he went into the army") settled into the familiar pattern of "postwar prosperity": a job with security, a home in the suburbs, lots of life insurance, kids to send to college. These values shaped the reality of my childhood; what had existed before became memory—except for that familiar catchphrase, both wonderful and sad: "until he went into the army." It symbolized the dramatic disruption of ordinary life and its return; the emergency and its abatement.

During the American Civil War, in the spring of 1864, Ralph Waldo Emerson contemplated the catastrophe around him: "The cannon will not suffer any other sound to be heard for miles and for years around it. Our chronology has lost all old distinctions in one date,—*Before the War, and since.*" Much the same could be said of World War II. The extraordinary moment absorbs the routine—then it, too, passes. But for my parents, their generation, years had been lost, and the routines, when they returned, no longer held the subliminal fires of possibility. My parents had envisioned something else, I think, "until he went into the army."

For me, too, the war was a great divide. "Until he went into the army" I have no memory of my father. (I was only eighteen months old.) He left behind half-filled ashtrays, which, because of some superstition, my mother refused to empty. They assumed an aromatic omnipresence that fascinated me. One morning, before my mother was awake, I accidentally broke his favorite green ceramic bowl, scattering the ashes. I recall my mother's anger. I also recall an unassuagable sadness. I remember being hoisted aboard a pony to have my picture taken to send to my father. More vividly, I can see him walking through the door in his uniform; I see myself standing in my crib watching him open the door.

What does it mean to be a war baby?

Prodded by my questions, my mother leads me down to the now-quiet basement, climbs over boxes of dusty tools, and yanks open a heavy metal drawer of my father's file cabinet. She has been here before. Now she extracts a bulging folder of correspondence. For six months, from May to November 1945, she sat each day at the wooden table in her cramped kitchen in the Bronx, not five minutes away from all the addresses she had ever known in her thirty-four years, and wrote anxious letters to my father, while the Army Air Corps shipped him from Mississippi to Illinois to Kansas to Nebraska, always threatening a destination overseas. Like most correspondents, my mother wrote about what she knew best: her family (mostly my sister and me) and her fears, "war nerves." She suffered from chronic nausea. "I sound like an idiot in those letters," she says, handing them over to posterity.

The file holds a mirror to my earliest confusions—gropings at the language, varieties of misbehavior (running into the gutter, peeing on the floor), wondering why Grandma doesn't always have teeth—but through it all runs a constant pain: "Where's Daddy? Daddy a bad Daddy—went away in the army." In one letter my mother describes a baby's bewilderment when a parcel of clothes arrived by mail—"Daddy's shirt, Daddy's socks, Daddy's shoes. Where's Daddy?" He sent a self-made record on V-J Day and I played it until the grooves squeaked. She let me wear his ties, his hats. I dared to climb into "Daddy's chair."

The loss was not merely symbolic. My sister, who was seven years older, apparently knew a different father, a hot-tempered, driven man who demanded obedience and perfection. Her letters to him were sad chronicles of piano lessons and practicing, suffused with guilt and promises to improve. His absence spared me such turmoil. He was not there to defy. And the war changed him, matured him. Perhaps because it was too late anyway, he expected less of me, accepted less. He would tolerate my petty delinquencies, even take a certain pride in my disrespect for other adults, teachers, authority in general. Later, he confessed embarrassment at his former self. Yet I never heard him express any fondness for his days in the army, and he came to love my mother's cooking.

"The War Is Over," she wrote to him upon learning the news. "What should I make for supper?"

What does it mean to be a war baby?

The question haunts me as my mother and I sit in a California living room and watch the black-and-white movie *The Best Years of Our Lives,* Hollywood's most popular offering of 1946. The hero, played by Frederic March, unexpectedly returns home from the war. His son sees him first, as I did my father, but before the boy can shout, his father places a hand on his mouth. The daughter (Teresa Wright) appears, but she stifles her cry. Then the children back away, allowing their mother (Myrna Loy) to rush into the foyer. They watch their parents embrace until, embarrassed, they go to their rooms. The lump thickens in my throat; my eyes well up. I've seen this movie a million times, and it always happens that way.

My obsession with *Best Years* resonates (uncomfortably) with

Freud's primal scene: the son displaced by the father's return. Have I imagined it? My mother assures me it was so. In the summer of 1945 my father was heading toward Japan. He had sent my mother a farewell gift, a shell necklace. By the time it arrived, the atom bomb had incinerated Hiroshima. The war was over. I remember my mother crying as she opened the package. Only hours later, from my crib in the bedroom, I could see my father open the door and come inside. He was thirty; I was two.

My memory draws me back to the movie. The parallel is no coincidence. From my subjective experience I can discern a broader historical dimension, an emotional reality, that elevates Hollywood's melodrama to the status of documentary. It's easy to disparage the romance of the silver screen; after all, Frederic March and Myrna Loy were actors, paid to perform. But after we allow for theatrical contrivances, what remains is utterly authentic: the *feeling* of the time. In *Best Years* the mood is halting, cautious, worried. Men who have felt the thrill of life, who have killed, shall once again become bankers and soda jerks. To see these characters alive on the screen, exactly as my parents would have seen them, establishes a time-defying presence. Even if they are not real as people, they are real as actors, no different in black and white than the subjects of newsreels. In fact, because the documentary films of World War II were unabashedly "message" films —propaganda—they tended to disguise certain unpleasant emotional truths. (John Huston's realistic portrayal of disabled war veterans, for example, *Let There Be Light,* was not released until 1981.) Hollywood did join the war effort, but the usual preoccupation with profits encouraged the industry to project an emotional common denominator that clings to the reruns. In this way Hollywood created a unique historical archive: a mood, an ambience that could have been preserved in no other way.

But to see the same movie forty years later is to see something else, too. For the "lessons" of history have intervened. The ambience has changed. What is self-evident in the original— things filmed inadvertently as background—emerges later as historical revelation: over time the invisible is rendered obvious. Several blacks appear in *Best Years,* for example, but only as nonspeaking shadows: soldier, chauffeur, dishwasher, jazz musician, washroom attendant; in the kitchen, mother and daughter shell fresh peas; the young son knows more than his father does about the atom bomb. These are silent artifacts in themselves, museum pieces, but like other historical facts, they illuminate unspoken assumptions about how a society functions, what keeps it together, and what it considers important. Implicit in this movie are the cultural roots, the foundations, upon which my generation —the war babies—would grow.

Consider only the title, *The Best Years of Our Lives*. "I gave you the best years of my life." That is what the peroxide blonde (Virginia Mayo) tells the air corps hero, her husband (Dana Andrews). ("Did you hear about the soldier who said he gave the best years of his *wife* to the Army?" my mother wrote to my father. "How true.") Then the bad blonde grabs her coat and walks out the door with another good-time Charlie. My mother, who claims she never dreamed of a divorce, blames the breakup of the American family on my generation. Virginia Mayo suggests otherwise. Not that the movie portrays her as a nice woman. After all, she'd worked in sleazy nightclubs while her clean-cut husband was busy blowing up Germany. She also complained about giving up her job after the war. She missed the glamour of night life; she wanted to supplement his civilian income so they could "have" things. When she walks out of the apartment, she disappears from the picture, leaving the Hollywood hero free to pursue a "good" woman (March's daughter, Teresa Wright). But even this good woman has already worked as a nurse, and so is not exactly innocent of the facts of life. In fact, she shocks her parents by vowing to destroy the Mayo-Andrews marriage. ("It's killing his spirit," she says.) That by the end of the movie she gets her man is not an unimportant point, especially considering the moral strictures that governed the film industry.

When I mention these subjects to my mother, I'm astonished at what she does not see: so many parallels to her own life. I bait her, asking her opinion of that "nice" Virginia Mayo. She answers by reflex: "Ugh." I try to persuade her that Virginia Mayo portrayed a not-uncommon reality at the war's end. Her desire to keep her job—the essence of the bad woman—mirrored the public-opinion polls of 1945. Although millions of women were abruptly laid off, most managed to find other jobs, setting an accelerating trend that eventually swept up my mother as well. By the mid-1950s she'd gotten a job—a "woman's" job in a department store—and she stayed in the work force until her retirement twenty years later.

"You were already grown up when I went to work," she says defensively.

"That's my point. I was eleven."

"I didn't need the money. Dad always paid for the household."

"But you liked the independence, didn't you?"

"It was nice to get out of the house."

That she was a wife and mother, that her work was optional, that her career was always secondary to my father's fits perfectly with the historical model of the postwar period. Yet my mother does not wish to be associated with this pattern. It threatens her image as "homemaker." Nor does she wish to be reminded of the obvious relationship between women working and the disruptions of the traditional family.

"You see," I say, trying to make her see, "it didn't start with my generation."

For a second her certainty falters, and I take the opportunity to introduce her to some statistics that do not exactly speak for themselves:

Year	Divorces per thousand
1910	83
1920	171
1930	196
1940	264
1945	485
1950	385
1955	377
1960	393
1965	479

"Notice the bulge in 1945," I say triumphantly. "Who's fault is that?"

Despite what I consider impressive numbers, however, my mother claims she cannot remember a single person of her age who was divorced.

"What about my aunt from Connecticut?" I ask.

"Oh, she's different. She was married so young."

"What about the lady across the alley?"

"Ugh, her. She was a tramp."

"What about all those Hollywood marriages?"

"Hollywood!"

"What about your sister-in-law's sister?"

"He was a bum."

"What about Joe's aunt and his brother's wife?"

"I didn't know them then."

I could go on like that, and so could she. By now, we're both exhausted by my history lesson. I'm only suggesting that her generation nurtured mine, that the war had social consequences long after 1945, that the sexual revolution, the divorce boom, and women's liberation did not occur mysteriously overnight. She has a glazed look in her eyes. But suddenly my mother notices the lower half of my chart:

1966	499
1967	523
1968	584
1969	639
1970	708
1975	1,036
1980	1,189

"Never mind," she exclaims, running a finger down the columns. "Those are your friends, not mine." Her eyes brim with pride. Once again, she's beaten the odds.

To talk about "generations" exaggerates our differences. So much time overlaps. For nearly half a century my mother and I have shared a common history—the war, the cold war, the Vietnam War, the moral equivalent of war; ten presidents and forty-odd Miss Americas. We've been influenced by the same public events; and about them we've agreed more times than not. Lately, we've

learned to depend on each other for this feeling of continuity—
mine backward, hers forward. Beyond heritage and genealogy, we
form a community in time.

I had always believed there was something unique about my
generation. Maybe everyone feels that way. Having been born
during the war, rather than before it, meant everything to me.
Unlike my mother and her contemporaries, I was acutely aware
that I was a product of the war, that I'd lived my entire life under
the shadow of its legacy: the realization, the consciousness, that
whole societies could be destroyed—methodically, the way the
Nazis exterminated the Jews of central and eastern Europe; impulsively, as Harry S Truman put it, by "harnessing the basic
power of the universe." That reality seemed to distinguish my
peer group.

Through the 1950s our teachers reminded us that ours was the
first generation never to know of peace. One war followed another.
The mushroom cloud became a cliché before it was a metaphor.
Visions of annihilation were never far from play or conversation:
take cover; be first on the block to drop the atom bomb. I still
own the dogtag from my second grade air-raid drills, and I recall
doubting, even then, its usefulness in identifying the corpse.

We were different. For us, the war babies, the future was always
precarious. It seemed to exist not as an extension of the present
but as something outside of time. Such a perspective shaped and
defined all our values and moral commitments. It's no wonder
that Tom Hayden launched the radical movement of the 1960s
with the phrase "We may be the last generation in the experiment
with living." To me it never sounded like hyperbole. The same
psychology—this elemental feeling of impermanence—may also
explain our tentative attitude toward social institutions: religion,
marriage, the family. Unlike our parents and grandparents, we've
always known the possibility of extinction. We've lived with the
knowledge that history could come to an end.

Given all those cosmic assumptions, I'm a little surprised we've
lasted so long. My expectations of disaster have failed to materi-
alize; maybe they never will. Once I turned forty and entered
the notorious "mid-life crisis," I could imagine, for the first time,

dying in my bed. At this age my preoccupations seem so much closer to those of my parents. I've become less concerned with some abnormal end of the world than with the pleasures and necessities of survival. I believe there's something precious to pass on, and I find myself imagining grandchildren playing under the table on the kitchen floor, listening.

FOUR

Homogenization

The scene encapsulated the conflicts of the 1960s: There, at the edge of a posh backyard swimming pool in southern California, stands the scion of postwar affluence—"the Graduate." As played by Dustin Hoffman in the 1967 movie, the Graduate is besieged by the values of the older generation. Their wisdom, passed along in the great oral tradition, is crushed into a single word—"Plastics!"—producing a moment of splendid hilarity that defined the notorious generation gap of the era. While the Graduate, personification of American youth, covets idealism —truth, sincerity, authenticity—his elders extol only the most indestructible form of material technology. Plastics, as they say, last forever.

But the same generation that transformed nonbiodegradable petrochemicals into icons of the American dream—my parents' generation, that is—had once been indoctrinated by Hollywood with similar pithy advice about survival in crisis times. The scene occurs, once again, in *The Best Years of Our Lives,* that harbinger of postwar anxiety. The character was called Homer, a latter-day Ulysses, and was played in the movie by Harold Russell, a real World War II veteran who had lost both his hands in a training accident and was showing his skill with artificial hooks. (Russell would be the only actor ever to win two Oscars for the same performance.) On his first day home his future in-laws express an understandable worry about Homer's ability to provide for their young daughter's future. The father mentions his concern about "another depression." Then he proposes a line of work well-suited for the postwar era—insurance.

Hollywood, as ever, had its finger on the American pulse. Although in the movie Homer ignores the fatherly advice (after all, he will receive weekly disability payments from Uncle Sam), insurance proved to be one of the great boom industries of the postwar period. Between 1950 and 1960 disposable family incomes increased by 49 percent, but sales of individual life insurance policies jumped by over 200 percent, a statistic that does not include the rise in employee benefit plans. Insurance also appeared as a recurring background device in numerous Hollywood films of the 1940s and 1950s—the subject of secondary dialogue, one of the major occupational categories (along with doctors, psychiatrists, and policemen), and a visual presence (on storefronts, for example) even when not part of the movie script. This enthusiasm for "insurance" seems to indicate a pervasive doubt about the future of the American economy, not to mention a prudent urge to protect whatever gains had been achieved. For all the contemporary boasting about "the affluent society"— later transcribed by television as "Happy Days"—the depression generation could never forget its origins.

So my family bought insurance. In 1947 my father put aside his hopes of becoming a symphonic composer, quit his temporary job with the post office, and became an eighth-grade music teacher in a New York City public school. The salary was modest —about $3,000 a year—but he was now a professional, worthy of his bachelor's degree and the white collar he wore. And the job provided the first occupational security—life insurance, in other words—he ever had.

Teaching proved to be my family's ticket into the middle class —the lower middle class, to be sure, but such distinctions were made only by academic sociologists. Soon we were imitating other upwardly mobile families in the Bronx, participating in the great surge of private consumption of durable commodities that prevented a return to hard times after the war. In 1948 we purchased our first automobile, a used Olds that had been owned by a disabled war veteran and had various gadgets, such as signal blinkers, attached to the steering wheel; the next year we got a floor-model Magnavox. Both had been equally unthinkable just a few years before. Some of our neighbors bought TV sets before their cars, but by 1950 everyone I knew owned one of those modern necessities. From my child's eye I never identified these purchases with economic advancement; they were something we obtained at a certain stage of development, a natural increment in the blessings of life. Like other kids, I became a sucker for favorite programs—"Howdy Doody" and "Captain Video" stick in my mind—as well as the products that sponsored them. Yet even though my age group well remembered the time before television, and therefore accepted restricted hours of viewing, the medium quickly became a currency of exchange, a cultural common denominator that all school children could share. The "Dragnet" theme song—Dum Da Dum Dum—seemed to transcend differences of region, race, and class.

This homogenization of kid culture would be accelerated by the rapid development of the suburbs. To historians the process is familiar: A postwar housing shortage inspired assembly-line geniuses, such as the builder William Levitt, to erect interchangeable residential units on the edges of big cities, resulting in the mass migration of interchangeable families into new communities where they formed a rootless, witless society summarized by the word *suburbia*. That geniuses like Mr. Levitt deliberately excluded black families from the subdivisions reinforced the middle-class sameness that social critics of the time deplored. But other geniuses—call them social scientists—were also at work. In what seems to be a recurring obsession in our recent history, middle-class families were becoming increasingly concerned about the sexual proclivities of American adolescents. Juvenile delinquency, teenage sex clubs, eventually the frenzied isometrics of Elvis the Pelvis, all revealed a subterranean power about to explode. To protect the innocent, as "Dragnet"'s Joe Friday might have put it, postwar educators rushed to restructure the academic environment. A separate institution of learning, known as the junior high school, would protect young adolescents from their older brothers and sisters.

When the local schools implemented the plan, my father had to transfer to a new junior high school in the boondocks of Queens. It was 1954, the peak of the urban exodus, but I wanted no part of the move. The very virtues of suburbia—trees and lawns, the lack of congestion—undermined my confidence. In the absence of paved sidewalks and curbs my street skills were worthless, and it felt utterly unnatural to chase a fly ball across grass. I was dazzled by the freedom of vacant lots and the burgeoning new construction that provided my new friends with all manner of building supplies to construct clubhouses and forts. In these opportunities for new kinds of play I felt only danger.

The social rules were also different. The ethnic composition, mostly Irish and Italian, put me in a distinct minority (and exposed me to my first contact with anti-Semitic prejudice), while the rapidly expanding black community nearby introduced a truly exotic ingredient. Recently, in doing research in some southern newspapers of the 1950s, I was surprised to find extensive coverage of crime waves in northern public schools; but this, I suspect, was primarily a projection of the editor's fears, especially in the wake of the *Brown* ruling that toppled the segregated school systems. Except for an occasional schoolyard brawl over who was safe or out, I recall no racial violence. In fact, most of my friends were self-consciously liberal in matters of race. I first heard the term *nigger* when I was ten, and not again until I was twelve, and both times it was a white person who silenced the bigot. Through high school blacks and whites played sports together, hung around the same candy stores to read *Superman* comic books, and went to the same house parties. (Interracial dating was something else.) Yet I was amazed to discover how few black faces appear in my high school yearbook. Did they simply skip the ceremonial photographs? Did they fail to graduate?

Disparities of wealth were also obvious, but they were remarkably unimportant—deliberately so—until we were almost old enough to drive cars. In New York you had to be eighteen. But friends who lived in the Tudor-style mansions of Jamaica Estates could afford special driving lessons and get their licenses a year earlier, leaving poorer kids and "cliff dwellers"—occupants of the low-income projects nearby—waiting at bus stops until we reached the magic age. On my seventeenth birthday I wrote the numbers 1 to 365 on a sheet of paper and assiduously crossed off the last number each day for a year. It seemed an eternity. But before that particular rite of passage differences in family incomes among my friends appeared slight. Because of peer pressure we all dressed with a contemporary uniformity—the "Ivy League" look of loden green, paisley, and khaki chinos—that declaimed a kind of military classlessness. Indeed, that particular uniformity —a civilian-soldier attire that went well with the military-style crew cuts of the 1950s—now seems a perfect mirror for the denial of class conflict that girded the cold war. Since I had no idea what most of my friends' parents did to earn a living, it was easy to declare—I remember fervently repeating this homily in a social studies class—that "in America we are all middle class."

Even the exceptions proved the rule.

On the evening the Russians launched the first sputnik in October 1957, my father and I were driving across the Fifty-ninth Street Bridge, and we passed the brightly lit United Nations building. "They kept the lights on late," my father observed. "They must be worried." It was his tone—"I told you so"—that troubled me. A few months later, while discussing the absurdity of Soviet propaganda—they were claiming to have invented the telephone—I said something sarcastic about communist dupes. We were sitting at the kitchen table, and my father shifted in his chair to face me. The corners of his mouth were about to break into a grin. "You should know," he warned, "that your father was a Red." He might have punched me in the stomach.

I took small comfort in his use of the third-person past tense (it had nothing to do with *me!*) and dared not mention the subject for months. When I did, he was defensive—admitting he had remained in the party after the Stalin-Hitler pact of 1939, even after World War II. He made no effort to justify his position. Besides, it was obvious that he was now a respected, satisfied member of the capitalist middle class. So I assumed that communism was merely a part of his youth, somewhere between childish and naïve, and that he was as embarrassed as I was by the past. In any case, it seemed safer—politically, psychologically— to let the matter rest. I was terrified that someone might find out. Only much later did I discover the unspoken legacies of being a red-diaper baby.

Besides security and respectability, my father's schoolteaching brought us an unfamiliar comfort. After a few more years of apartment living and much borrowing, my parents managed to buy a small forty-year-old frame house in Flushing. The place had up-to-the-minute white aluminum siding but needed plenty of fixing. Despite two grandfathers in the building trades and the fact that my father could do anything with his hands—maybe because of it—I showed no aptitude for home repair. My usual modus operandi was twofold: (1) break tool; (2) cut hand. I was soon assigned to the ignominious task of sweeping up after the work was done. When my father installed a wood-paneled wall in the living room, I succeeded in applying a rich and lustrous stain over about three quarters of the surface. Then, for reasons I no longer remember, perhaps a call to play catch, I walked away from the job, leaving it as it was. They lived in that house for twenty years, but no one ever asked why the color of the wood changed abruptly at eye level. They didn't need to ask. Still, I loved that house, the luxury of my own room overlooking the tree-lined street; the fifty-foot Bing cherry tree that lured me into its branches each June; especially the walk-in closets in the basement that shielded me from scrutiny and protected my guilt.

Among my father's many books was a child's garden of sin— an unhidden shelf of sexual subjects, which ranged from Krafft-Ebing's two-volume *Pyschopathia Sexualis* to some un-Latinized samples of low-life pornography. These I perused daily after school in the solitude of my closets. My father and I talked about sex a great deal—he was always trying to make me blush—but never once discussed those books. I suppose he read them for the same reason I did—for glimpses of forbidden possibilities. When a group of my high-school friends chipped in and rented an evening's worth of blue movies, he expressed mild disappointment at missing the show. (The father in whose home we screened the films proudly occupied a front-row seat!) Yet my father's fantasies seem to have been largely unconsummated. Historians now see those postwar years as a time of male crisis —the beginnings of a postindustrial age when men abandoned the rigors of the private marketplace in favor of bureaucratic jobs requiring gray flannel suits, became "organization" men, and simultaneously saw a new breed of independent women challenge the economic basis of the traditional patriarchy. One result, as Dr. Alfred Kinsey so well documented, was a rise in adultery and other extracurricular pasttimes. Knowing about such trends, my father felt doubly frustrated. But his interest in sex never implied permissiveness. He was a great flirt—blunt, vulgar, funny— but vastly inexperienced. A decade later, he would be surprised, then envious at the sexual revolution. What I learned from him— all the candor notwithstanding—was that sexual frustration was not unnatural, that the best remedy was marriage, and that the sooner it was done the better.

But while my father defended the sexual status quo, he tolerated—no stronger verb is possible—other kinds of experimentation. He was a musician first, a longhair, and he had insisted I study a musical instrument (the trumpet, as it turned out) with an eye to becoming a concert performer. I certainly had the talent, but my ambition was nil, my self-discipline less. I was also horrified by the idea of seeming square. At a time when most American teenagers were gobbling up rock and roll, forcing the new sound into the collective consciousness, the idea of playing classical music was equivalent to speaking Latin. I rebelled through jazz. It was neither classical nor junk, and it required a genuine virtuosity—skill, technique, rapture. With a few equally maladjusted friends, I became a regular at Birdland, the jazz emporium at Broadway and Fifty-second Street, where for two bucks we could hear Miles Davis, Dizzy Gillespie, or Maynard Ferguson set the mirrored walls shaking. For another buck we could buy a Coke and spike it with the rye whiskey we carried around in small liquid-vitamin bottles. We were sixteen years old.

It was not just the music that pulled me to jazz. In the dark and smoky nightclubs of mid-Manhattan and the Village, I found alternatives to the suburban dream. Gillespie, higher than a kite, would perform marvelous impersonations of racist southern governors or leap into a falsetto voice to mock the transvestite stage announcer. Interracial couples, homosexuals, pot-smoking drummers: they seemed pretty normal when they spoke. Once a goateed engineering student gave me a copy of Allen Ginsberg's *Howl,* and I marveled to see the word *fuck* in print, as in "America go fuck yourself with your atom bomb." After midnight we would head for the subway phone booths to make long-distance telephone calls on a stolen credit card to such places as the Hotel Thomas Jefferson in Birmingham, Alabama, just to ask, "What is your policy on Negroes?" and hoot at the answer, "Certainly not!"

If our dissidence now seems indistinguishable from petty delinquency, the reverse is also true. Beyond the conformity of suburbia, the consensus politics of the Eisenhower years, and the prevailing values of the prospering middle class, I had discovered a fascinating underworld of possibility. I was too young, too cautious, too straight to embrace this way of life or, to be honest, to be accepted by the hipsters and beatniks I admired. They became, in the end, part of my fantasy world—romantic nonconformists who could thrive creatively in spite of, because of, their distance from people like my parents.

Where I got such positive notions about Bohemia I do not know. Temperamentally I was conservative to the core, fearful of standing out or excelling in any way. I wanted nothing more than approval from the world I inherited. When I graduated from high school in 1960, just a few weeks before John Kennedy summoned the nation toward new frontiers, my life reflected the mediocrity of America's white middle-class youth. I won no prizes, had no plans. I just managed to squeak into the local municipal college, but a career was as remote to me as a steady girlfriend. Yet I held an underlying confidence, so much was I a product of the times, that wife and success would arrive with the same inevitability. And with those attributes—family, position, success—I would also acquire all the other tangible benefits of the dream: material possessions, security, insurance; in short, plastics.

FIVE

The Getaway

Politics encroached on me slowly. When and how it happened seem less important questions than where. For the setting determined the content. While my richer friends went to out-of-town colleges, and the poorer ones did not go to college at all, I enrolled at Queens College in Flushing because I was there, it was cheap, they accepted me, and consequently I did not have to make any other choices.

In the autumn of my freshman year the New York Yankees lost a seven-game World Series to the Pittsburgh Pirates, a defeat not quite offset the next month by the victory of John F. Kennedy over Richard Nixon. Far more than both was I interested in an October birthday present from my sister, a subscription to *Playboy* magazine, though I now can see certain similarities between the air-brushed images designed by Hugh Hefner and those projected by the Democratic candidate. What attracted me to Kennedy was the celebrated "style": the president smoking a black cigar at the Army-Navy game, sailing on the *Honey Fitz*, married to that breathless woman. Whatever Hefner was dangling as the American dream—sex, money, power—Kennedy had attained.

Slickness rather than intellectual achievement was my aspiration. Given such priorities, it was appropriate that my higher education began with a class called Elementary Basketball, where

I studied ambidextrous dribbling. Before my next class I had a two-hour break, which I spent in the student lounge smoking Marlboros and checking out the female scene with another un-ambitious friend. We wore pullover sweaters and ties, sported "Madison Avenue" haircuts, and strove to be collegiate. Mostly we blew smoke. In our third week of this ritual we were interrupted by one of his friends, a more serious scholar, who announced that he was going to join the staff of the student newspaper, the *Phoenix*. He urged us to come.

The *Phoenix* (aptly named after the mythological bird that rose from the ashes) occupied the last remaining space in the base-ment of a half-demolished building waiting for its final execution. The first impression was of siege, a wobbly feeling that the entire structure would suddenly groan and turn to shambles. Decades earlier, someone had painted the walls lime green, but long ago the color had faded and been adorned by esoteric graffiti. The furniture was ancient—desks without drawers, armless chairs, crochety typewriters, and a single torn leather chair that was forever occupied by a sleeping student. Over the years, one four-drawer file cabinet had been filled to capacity with empty beer cans, and it emitted an unabated sour odor. Prudently—because you should write only about what you know—I applied to the sports department and was assigned, no questions asked about my competence, to cover a junior varsity soccer game, which un-fortunately was scheduled for the same time as my French class. True to form, I cut the class and filed the story.

It was not journalism that elicited such commitment, how-ever, but the wacky spirit that filled the basement office. Here, in a literal underground, I had stumbled upon the student avant-garde, such as it was in 1960. Older students—sophomores, say—were forever discussing theater, jazz, or psychoanalysis. Pre-tension prevailed, though at first I confused it with brilliance. The more arcane the vocabulary, the more obscure the literary allusion, the more profane the poetry, the greater the prestige. I never understood what anyone was talking about. But what was thrilling and instantly seductive was the intensity of argument—and the political implications. Should we endorse Kennedy?

Should we picket Woolworth's (their lunch counters in the South denied service to Negroes)? Should Communists be allowed to speak on the campus?

Queens College had a reputation as the "Little Red Schoolhouse." During the McCarthy years, one of the deans had refused to surrender student files to the FBI and was harassed from his post. The Brooklyn *Tablet,* a Catholic diocese rag, regularly attacked such communist influences, and three associate professors, claiming a bias against Catholics, were suing the administration for failing to promote them. The college was understandably touchy about Reds. An official speaker policy banned anyone indicted under the antisubversive Smith Act, lest our tender minds be swayed. On these grounds the administration denied a podium to Gus Hall, head of the Communist party, and refused to let students hear the lyrics of Pete Seeger. The mentality presumed subversion everywhere; without discipline there would be anarchy. So during my first semester, the dean ordered that any female wearing long pants or shorts be expelled from classes.

The newspaper office soon stood in the eye of the storm. Late in the summer of 1961, around the time President Kennedy announced the resumption of atmospheric tests of nuclear bombs, one of the editors returned from the annual convention of the National Students Association clutching three Latin words: "in loco parentis." As we sat on the old metal folding chairs in the basement office, he explained this ancient scholastic concept— the words translated "in the place of parents"—as an attack on our rights as free individuals. Under cover of in loco parentis, college administrators could—and did—treat us as children, defining and limiting our freedom to act and think. We were very impressed by his presentation, and we resolved to pursue the matter. The first editorial of the year announced our cautious attack on the doctrine of in loco parentis: "We will not rant and rave about our rights but we will assert our responsibility." Which meant, I think, that we would show ourselves to be sufficiently mature to monitor our own behavior—our social events, political clubs, extracurricular activities—in the interests of the whole "academic community"; we would prove our worth as company men. Yet the final sentence of that editorial established unmistakably the direction of the decade: "We will kill *in loco parentis*."

Big talk from the little man. Two weeks after the editorial appeared, the administration banned a speaker invited by the student Marxism Discussion Club, Benjamin Davis, secretary of the CP, and then disinvited Malcolm X, apparently because the Black Muslim leader was traveling around under an alias. What could we do? With the slogan, "Ban the Ban," we organized a one-day boycott of classes. Someone handed me a picket sign that said STRIKE TODAY, and I joined a few hundred students parading around the quadrangle to protest the speaker ban. On assignment from my editor, I also entered one of the classrooms to count student attendance and was promptly thrown out by a furious teacher for violating his academic freedom. Remarkably, the strike succeeded. According to our head count, about two-thirds of the students skipped classes that day—presumably for a principle. The *New York Times* published an editorial about the "right to listen"; prominent liberal columnists of the New York dailies endorsed us. We were elated: We had shown our strength, proven our moral advantage. What did it mean?

Among our coconspirators was a quiet fellow named Robert Savio. Three years later, another Savio—Mario Savio—emerged as a leader of the Free Speech Movement at the University of California's Berkeley campus, exhorting students to throw their bodies on the gears of the bureaucratic machinery. And Berkeley sparked the student movement of the decade: protests against patriarchal college administrators, racial injustice, the draft, the Vietnam War. It became the granddaddy of widespread campus dissent: Columbia, People's Park, Kent State, and hundreds of other less famous rebellions. It ignited the demand for empowerment, and it led, belatedly, to the constitutional amendment lowering the voting age to eighteen. How did our little incident at Queens College relate to these larger events? It was a dozen years before I learned that Bob and Mario Savio were one and the same.

Besides that historical footnote, the strike at Queens was significant mainly for what it did not accomplish. The speaker policy there did not change, and we had exhausted our alternatives. Back we went to writing editorials and suffering through interminable meetings with college officials. In these bureaucratic corridors our movement died, a victim of talk. For although we considered ourselves student radicals, we did not seek to change the structure of political authority on campus; all we really wanted was acceptance into the adult world.

We were treated, nonetheless, as enemies of the state. Our subsequent editorial attack on the House Un-American Activities Committee (HUAC) reawakened the anger of the Catholic *Tablet* and resulted in the college president summoning the entire editorial board to his office at the crack of dawn. We knew what was coming; in anticipation, we had all gotten drunk the night before. Now, with burning hangovers, we marched into the carpeted conference room and took seats around a long, polished wood table. At the head sat the college president, a man whose gray hair parted precisely at the center of his scalp. He was wearing rimless eyeglasses, a dark wool suit, white shirt, and tie, as usual, and, as usual, he was not smiling. Without a word of greeting he nodded to his secretary, who walked around the table and handed each of us an envelope with each name typed on the front. Careful as any corporation lawyer, I slipped out the typed page and read my letter, and then refolded the page and placed it back in the envelope. It was a document I knew I would always treasure. The college president had placed each of us on disciplinary probation. Then, in the most earnest voice he could muster, he explained that the college was "a going concern"; we were mere transients who had no claims on company policy. He also assured us that he was our friend, that more powerful figures wanted to see us permanently expelled. And he warned us, under threat of expulsion, not to comment editorially on this ruling.

As a testament to our fear, we accepted the verdict. We did not protest; we did not even complain. For against the backdrop of liberal idealism about the youth of America—Kennedy's Peace Corps, the space program, the budding civil rights movement—we wanted to protect our tickets to the beneficent future. Nothing better illustrates the hopeful campus mood of the early 1960s than that plain, unselfish desire. We wanted, in other words, our college diplomas.

The simplicity of those expectations underlined not only our political inexperience but also the promise of the time—the same hubris that inspired President Kennedy to state that "most of the problems . . . we now face are technical problems, are administrative problems . . . very sophisticated judgments which do not lend themselves to the great sort of 'passionate movements' which have stirred the country so often in the past." As disciples of the president—good middle-class liberals—we believed that progress and reason were interchangeable terms. The attitude was best expressed in one of the more popular movies of the day, *Inherit the Wind,* about the Scopes "monkey trial" of the 1920s. In its relentless assault on religious superstition we could plainly see the better scientific future. With our college educations we wanted to become the cool technicians of the modern world. None of us doubted that this spirit would soon and inevitably prevail in Appalachia and Mississippi, not to mention Africa, Latin America, and Southeast Asia.

Our suspicion of what Kennedy called "great . . . passionate movements" also reflected a cold-war curriculum that persisted well into the 1960s. Among the more widely circulated books of my college years was an anthology written by ex-Communists, *The God That Failed,* subtitled "Why Six Great Writers Rejected Communism." Arthur M. Schlesinger, Jr., Kennedy's personal historian, had written a blurb for the back cover, giving the book a kind of official seal. "A faith is not acquired by reasoning," explained Arthur Koestler, one of the six. "One does not fall in love with a woman, or enter the womb of a church, as a result of logical persuasion. Reason may defend an act of faith—but only after the act has been committed." In this view, the infatuations of youth, whether sexual or ideological, supposedly would give way with maturity to a politics of reason. Yet all the writers acknowledged that acts of faith, because they were by definition irrational, could not easily be changed.

The essay by the journalist Louis Fischer, for example, described the ordeal of Alexander Berkman, who did not see the truth about communism until a traumatic event—the Bolsheviks' bloody suppression of a sailors' revolt on the island of Kronstadt —destroyed the illusions of Soviet ideology. "What counts decisively is the 'Kronstadt,'" said Fischer, meaning a historical shock that breaks one's connection to the entire body of belief. "I had no 'Kronstadt' for many years," he said. But once the Kronstadt came—in his case the Nazi-Soviet nonaggression pact of 1939— the carefully woven fabric of his religion fell apart. He suffered then what might be called an identity crisis. He lost his faith; or, more passively, the god had failed. Yet with a new truth it became possible to form new love relationships: the anticommunism of the cold war era. "'Kronstadt' is not a dead end," Fischer insisted. It had, instead, set him on course to a "conversion to the ideas of democracy."

Kronstadt, for my generation, was more subtle and slower to be understood, and yet ultimately it, too, was responsible for a powerful transformation of ideals and commitment. For college students who in 1961 promised not to "rant and rave about our rights" but instead to "assert our responsibility," the liberal faith disintegrated quickly after the assassination of President Kennedy.

"Kennedy's been shot," a classmate told me with a worried look on his face.

"That's good for Bobby in sixty-four," I replied. Then I realized what he had said.

To all my friends the assassination was, first, a psychological blow —a time-stopping event that moved in slow motion and yet instantly cut through our illusions about the sanctity of democratic institutions, the succession of the presidency, and government by consent. In the short run, Lyndon Johnson would exploit our grief and craving for consensus to push through civil rights legislation and the Great Society. But none of my friends considered him a legitimate president. *MacBird.* The title said it all. Here was born the infamous "credibility gap." I've always thought the most striking statistic of the decade was a Gallup poll taken in 1966 that showed that a majority of Americans did not believe the findings of the Warren Commission about the death of the president, and yet the same majority opposed a reopening of the case. Our politics would never be the same. Three gunshots in Dallas and an entire generation's civics lessons flew out the window.

On that very day I had expected to give a diamond ring to my fiancée, thus taking another uncautious step down the primrose path. Marriage was one more side of the middle-class dream, and it holds the key to understanding the immense cultural upheaval, or lack thereof, associated with the 1960s. For the liberal stirrings of that decade were played out against an unyielding backdrop of conventional expectations. Indeed, the most liberated of my college friends—those who resisted middle-class proprieties, rented pads in the Village, and experimented with sex, drugs, and lifestyles—were also the first to rush to the altar.

The appeal of marriage among young liberals was simple: It signified maturity; it provided a semblance of power and self-determination, often before the legal age of adulthood. As one of the most radical coeds I knew used to say, "It makes the fucking legal." Marriage meant sophisticated coupling, not families. It did not imply settling down forever, though cars, kids, and homes, in approximately that order, had a way of raising the ante. All that seemed remote. Even though we had been raised in the middle-class thralldom of the 1950s—"I Love Lucy," "Father Knows Best," "The Honeymooners," all were deliberately mistitled renditions of sexual combat—we expected to evade the banal stereotypes that had sentenced our parents' generation to a lifetime of responsibility.

Heather (as I shall call her) was seventeen and a college freshman when I first saw her drinking a glass of red wine at an unstaid Christmas party in the home of a mutual friend. She had straight brown hair with bangs, a spontaneous gap-toothed smile, and a pair of crinkly dimples just below her almond-shaped brown eyes. She wore gold hoop earrings, no makeup. She was small-boned but big-breasted, not exactly frail, and she smoked Marlboro cigarettes and swore and played the guitar and held it all together inside a black turtleneck sweater and blue jeans. She was talking breathlessly about hitchhiking through Europe in the summer, describing plans to follow the sun from Ireland to Crete in pursuit of the ancient secrets of the Minotaur. About which I knew nothing. The next time we met, at another house party, I slipped my hand under the black turtleneck sweater and was rewarded with a big kiss. What a surprise!

I tell these intimacies to evoke the mood—a feeling of imminence. Heather and I were both middle class, or so we thought. (Having been raised in the suburban 1950s, we lacked a vocabulary to distinguish the upper middles from the lowers, a difference that seemed important only later.) Her father, like mine, had opted for the civil service; both families were Jewish, equally enamored of education. Our courtship promised to fulfill all parental expectations. We made a nice couple.

But what attracted us was an essential unconventionality. Mostly I remember going to the movies, any and all—*Tom Jones,* James Bond, *8½*—because "film" was art; and then taking the subway into the Village for espresso or browsing among Marboro's remaindered books. We bought volumes we thought we should own: tiny illustrated editions of Matisse and Paul Klee, a biography of John Adams, collections of short stories by unknown authors. Heather introduced me to her folk music scene —the Clancy Brothers, Josh White, Odetta—and I taught her of Miles, Dizzy, and John Coltrane. I was reading Hemingway and Thomas Wolfe then, teeming novels about men growing up, and I was prowling for every new adjective to describe my feelings of awakening and the yearning to leave New York and get on with my life. I felt like a sprinter poised on the blocks. Say "bang," and I'd be gone.

That was the fantasy, the reality was somewhat different. I had no confidence; frankly, I was afraid to light out for the territories alone. And I was in love. But Heather also needed a getaway and a good driver. We conspired to escape together.

By then I was majoring in history. To be honest, other courses —literature, philosophy—aroused my curiosity far more, but history appealed most as a career. Who can say exactly why? Because the fossilized history department offered the easiest curriculum?

Because I had a good head for details? Because it was my sister's worst subject? All true. But also because I truly dreaded the toll of time and held a mournful desire to save the past from obliteration. I yearned to contain what seemed to be an inevitable rush toward oblivion. Of course, at that age I could not articulate such feelings. Instead, I defined my passion for the past in professional terms and resolved to study history in graduate school. Luckily, I was two years ahead of the baby boomers who would flood the graduate schools in the mid-1960s (partly to avoid the military draft). With my better-than-average grades (straight As in history), I had a choice of fellowships.

So I would leave New York for a better education, and Heather, as my wife, would transfer to the same university. We planned our wedding for the fall. (Kennedy's death merely postponed the engagement for a week.) We made our vows at Manhattan's Hotel Saint Moritz on a Saturday night; on Sunday I hit the ignition and we left, heading west.

PART TWO

Midpassage

Midwest

SIX

Insoluble Problems

Welcome to the Heartland. In the autumn of 1964 Heather and I landed in one of those peaceful, tree-lined college towns that sprouted around the Midwest in the middle of the last century. Here I would enroll in graduate school, and for the next four years render unto Clio, the muse of history, what Virginia Mayo called "the best years of my life." The local townfolk were rich and conservative, as were most of the students and faculty on the lake-front campus. Rental advertisements requested "white only"; sororities and fraternities routinely blackballed Jews. Among the more prominent civic institutions was the headquarters of the Women's Christian Temperance Union. You may imagine the difficulty in finding a place to buy a beer. In fact, there were none; the damn place was dry. Yet barely ten minutes from the heavy iron gates that separated campus from town slept the "hog butcher for the world," then run by Chicago's jowly mayor, Richard J. Daley.

Through all the tribulations of the 1960s I rested securely in the bosom of Clio, and so did most of my friends. Wrapped in the cloak of Scholarship, we devoted ourselves to the printed word: We memorized bibliographies, learned to distinguish schools of history writing, and practiced disputations about the arcane and the obscure. Meanwhile, we blithely permitted the real history of the times to pass us by. Nothing now embarrasses me more

than the discrepancy between what was going on in the sixties—
the history *of* the sixties—and the study of history *in* the sixties.
For none of the famous tumult of the streets made the slightest
indentation in the halls of academe.

So fully did the regimen of graduate school claim my attention in these years that it also absorbed any sense of a private
life. All my friends were colleagues, apprentice historians, and all
we discussed in our many drunken evenings and sober mornings
after were the skills of the trade, spiced abundantly with snide
gossip about our distinguished mentors. It was, in short, a closed
world—a man's world, too, not very different in its way from the
society of the locker room. Always, our wives and girlfriends remained outside—mildly amused, mildly impressed by the way we
took our work, ourselves, so seriously. I remember no voice ever
raised in dissent. That was because life in this cloister appeared
only tentative, a trial to be endured and overcome before a more
"real" life could begin. The prime casualty of that illusion was my
marriage—nearly all our marriages, as it turned out—though it
would take many years for me to realize how and why it happened
that way.

Heather and I had rented a university-run "furnished efficiency apartment," which was a euphemism for one room, galley
kitchen, closet, and bath, as well as a convertible couch with in-
curable lumps and a wooden table that once had been scorched
by a runaway electric iron. "I'm trying to think big," Heather
wrote to her parents the first night. She promptly began to de-
velop schemes for home improvement. Heather had not expected
the worst. We were living on my two-hundred-dollar-a-month
fellowship, nearly half of which went for rent, and despite two
sweaty summer jobs in New York we lacked the savings to improve our circumstances. Here was Heather, nineteen years old
(I was twenty), all grown up, a woman, a wife, stuck in a residential hotel nicknamed Fertile Acres because of the propensity of
student wives to get pregnant. She dreaded the prospect.

Still an undergraduate, she got a part-time job typing faculty
paperwork, and she dispensed her dismal paychecks on bright-
colored curtains that hung from brass rods, an unportable AM

radio, and the mild-mannered goldfish I called Elmer. Such humble acquisitions merely fed her frustrations. Insurance, that demon of the middle classes, meant we couldn't afford a car, so Heather borrowed a bike and cruised the neighborhood until she found larger quarters. It was a "partially furnished" flat in the basement of an old Victorian house owned by two widowed sisters-in-law. The younger was eighty-five and sharp as a tack, which probably is why she permitted the senile one to become the business manager. At least twice a month the poor thing would come to collect the rent—$120 a month as I recall—which, of course, had already been paid. "My husband used to be a music professor," she would begin every conversation in a wavering voice, and Heather's eyes would glaze over as she contemplated this embodiment of our academic future.

We lived in the basement for a couple of years, long enough to cherish sunlight. After her graduation, Heather found secretarial work, which enabled us to occupy a better habitat. She bought another batch of curtains, Japanese floor mats, and a couple of rare pieces of Carnival glass. "Just because we're poor," she used to say, "doesn't mean we have to live like we're poor." After a brief stint in nursing school, Heather put her career on hold and plunged into more direct forms of gratification: Shoes were the first thing I noticed; haircuts, no lie, at The Ritz. Worse were the gifts she gave me, which usually were another form of home improvement. A valet, for example. No, not a polite man with a French accent, but a piece of wood with a cushion to sit on while removing one's socks, a tray in which to place odd coins that collect in the cuffs, and a hanger-type projection on which the gentleman might place his coat and trousers. Here I was, wearing the same outfit, pardon the expression, seven days a week, shaving about every third day, getting haircuts every six months whether I needed one or not, with a valet to keep my study tidy.

We did not use the phrase "class warfare," but I soon discovered that our disagreements about conspicuous consumption made for a nice spectator sport. Most of my classmates were single men, and they reveled in my discomforts. I was named "Sambo," after the happy-go-lucky stereotype who walked the rooms saying

"Yas'm, yas'm." The strange thing was that I considered myself happily married. The idea of the wife going on a shopping binge, overdrawing the checking account, owning a dozen pair of shoes all seemed natural. Besides, I was content to let Heather take charge of the home front. I was too busy to care, glad she had something to occupy her time. The fact is, I knew she could take care of me better than I could ever manage, even with the valet. And that, ironically, became the main source of her pride.

This unquestioning acceptance of personal adversity mirrored our response to the political world outside. We were not ignorant of the news, nor emotionally unaffected. As with the Kennedy assassination, I remember exactly where I was when I first learned about the bombing of North Vietnam, the explosion in Watts, the landing of U.S. Marines in Danang, Bloody Sunday in Selma, Alabama, the march on the Pentagon, Khe Sanh and the Tet offensive—the hideous list seems endless—the murders of Martin Luther King and Robert F. Kennedy, the Democratic National Convention of 1968. And we remained liberals, saw ourselves as informed dissenters. We occasionally took risks. We signed petitions opposing the war, joined a demonstration protesting Secretary of State Dean Rusk's appearance on campus, and once wrote letters to our congressman to complain about the violations of civil rights in Mississippi. I got my first and only traffic ticket for daring to drive in Chicago with a Eugene McCarthy bumper sticker.

Such minimal involvement, at most a hesitant indignation, contributed to a developing political conscience. In retrospect, I can see in the unfolding crises—the headline history of the 1960s— a steady erosion of political faith; each public shock seemed to weaken my attachment to the system. I remember, for example, the terrific anxiety when for the first time at Wrigley Field in Chicago I did not stand up for the playing of the "Star Spangled Banner"; I remember, too, the surrounding fury. By contrast, I let tears run down my cheeks when Pete Seeger brought the entire audience at Orchestra Hall to its feet to sing "We Shall Overcome." These were small steps, tokens of awakening, but the process assumed a certain inexorability: private feelings moving gradually, relentlessly from exasperation to a sense of betrayal, from disgust to rage. I was heading toward my Kronstadt—my moment of political conversion.

But then it did not happen that way, at least on the surface.

I was preoccupied instead with my call, the urge to think historically. Or to put it another way, I was possessed with a fascination with the dead. Obsessively I read the prefaces of old books with the same interest some people give to the obituaries in the newspapers. They always referred to friends and helpers, wives who typed and children who kept quiet, and in the old books, I knew, all the loved ones were dead. Why was this morbidity rattling around in my skull? Blame it on the Holocaust, the atom bomb, the endless war in Vietnam. Understand my loneliness. I wanted to defy time, bring the past into the land of the living.

So despite the ordeal of my historical apprenticeship, what sociologists call professionalization, and despite its numbing effect on my marriage and my political instincts, I was lured into History, enticed by the mystery of the craft, by the endless unraveling of veils and the elegant beauty I imagined beneath. How else can I say it? I fell in love with Clio. This is how it began.

It's the last Monday afternoon of September 1964. A small, gray-haired man wearing a business suit, white shirt, and tie strides into the paneled seminar room and seats himself in the large, armed chair at the head of the long table. He peers over his tortoiseshell bifocals at the dozen young graduate students, who try to look smart. He has a bemused look on his face and he can barely utter a sentence without interjecting a nervous "huh, huh, huh." "Half of you won't be here next September," he says with a chuckle. "The remainder of you will be friends for the rest of your lives."

That was the first day. Uncle Frank, as we came to call our renowned professor (among ourselves, of course), proceeded to elaborate a plan by which we would soon ascertain whether we really wanted to enter the historical profession, and as he put it, "huh, huh, huh," whether the feeling would be mutual. Then he distributed a list of research topics, one of which we were to choose as our own. He called them "Insoluble Problems": each one raised a historical question that, because of the sheer absence of information, would be impossible to answer. He was interested in our techniques of research, our discipline and tenacity, rather than the qualities of imagination or intellect.

WHO WERE THE SURVIVORS OF CUSTER'S LAST STAND?
WHO EXPLODED THE BOMB AT HAYMARKET SQUARE?
WHO BUILT THE NEWPORT TOWER?
WHO CARVED THE KENSINGTON RUNE STONE?
WHO WAS PRESTER JOHN?

In the spirit with which quiz-show contestants used to answer Groucho Marx's consolation question, "Who is buried in Grant's tomb?" I chose the title WHERE WAS THE BATTLE OF SARATOGA FOUGHT? How obscure could that be?

I listened impatiently as Uncle Frank proceeded to hand out long lists of bibliographic guides, which he called "The Indispensables"—bibliographies of bibliographies, historical dictionaries and encyclopedias, atlases, maps, and gazeteers. He dictated the "correct" form of taking notes—five-by-eight-inch sheets of sixteen-pound typing paper cut to specifications with ample margins for cross-references, indexes, and short-form footnoting. He explained how bibliographic notes work best on three by fives: author (last name first), title, city, publisher, edition, date, and call number (in pencil, in case you had to find the book again). These formats obviously required elaborate organizing principles, and soon we were all buying those ugly black-and-white cardboard boxes in sizes 3" x 5", 5" x 8", 8½" x 11". (Later, I discovered that Uncle Frank's rules were amateurish compared to the professor who insisted we submit papers with margins of twenty and seventy, with precisely twenty-five double-spaced lines to a page; any other format meant the paper went unread!) With such training we would all become little obsessive-compulsives, hoarding and organizing, hoarding and organizing.

After I made a few false starts, a friendly librarian introduced me to *The Dictionary of American History,* one of the Indispensables, and I quickly located all the relevant information about the

Battle of Saratoga. After a brief skirmish at Bennington, Vermont, on August 16, 1777, General Burgoyne "pushed south to the region of Saratoga, and on September 19 attacked the Americans at Freeman's Farm. . . . He renewed his attack on October 7, and this time was badly beaten and forced to surrender (October 17, 1777)." That was it. The Battle of Saratoga was fought at Freeman's Farm *near* Saratoga. Surely this was the fastest solution to any of Uncle Frank's Insoluble Problems!

"That can't *possibly* be it," shrieked an older graduate student when I boasted about how quickly I had solved an Insoluble. First of all, he yelled, looking over my notes, I had neglected to write down the page number on which I had found the precious information.

"I'll go back tomorrow and get it," I suggested, feeling only a mite deflated.

"Let me tell you something else," he said, calming down. It seems I had used the wrong size of notepaper; worse, I had written the bibliographic data (incomplete though it was) on the back of footnote paper. "Uncle Frank does not like that." He went on to tell the story of another equally careless graduate student who had made a similar blunder the year before for which his grade had been lowered, which cost him his fellowship, which nearly wiped him out of the program. When I had absorbed these elemental points, he dropped the bomb: "Uncle Frank would never assign such a simple-minded question." My friend made no claims to know the correct answer to the question WHERE WAS THE BATTLE OF SARATOGA FOUGHT? "I could give a shit" is how he put it. But he offered to bet a million dollars it wasn't going to be found in *The Dictionary of American History!*

Back at the *Dictionary* I found additional cross-references, from which I learned that Burgoyne, after capturing Fort Ticonderoga in July 1777, had chased the retreating Americans through Hubbardton, Skenesborough (now Whitehall), and Fort Ann, and then encountered the forces of General Horatio Gates "entrenched at Bemis Heights, about eight miles south of the Hamlet of Saratoga, now Schuylerville. . . . The first battle of Freeman's Farm was fought September 19." More than a little confused, I found yet another cross-reference to "Freeman's Farm, First Battle of," which began: "Freeman's Farm . . . also known as . . . Bemis Heights, or Stillwater." I began to wonder if "the Hamlet of Saratoga" was a place or a person. Was I destined, like Burgoyne's beleaguered army, to march through dense thickets and hidden entrenchments unto defeat?

Had I better understood the rules of scholarship, I would have moved promptly toward one of those historical gazeteers that abounded on Uncle Frank's list of Indispensables. In my ignorance, something else, more wonderful, happened. I allowed my mind to wander across the familiar place-names from my childhood: Fort Ticonderoga, where one summer my parents took me to see the historical museum and walk through the guardhouse that once held patriot prisoners of war—it had smelled of cooked cabbage that day; Whitehall (called Skenesborough in the 1770s), where we shopped for groceries at the Grand Union and I impressed the checkout lady by whistling through a missing tooth; Lake George in the Adirondacks, purportedly "the second purest water in the world," where I caught my first sunfish and called myself Ethan Allen while leading my Green Mountain Boys onto one of its birch-dense islands. Swept by such memories, I lingered over the entry "Ticonderoga, Taken by Burgoyne" and read how King George III, so exultant in the victory, had exclaimed "I have beat them! I have beat all the Americans!"

Moved in this way, I perused the cross-references of the region. Under "Ticonderoga, Capture of" there was the story of Henry Knox, a mere twenty-four years old, who took charge of transporting 119,000 pounds of ordnance from Fort Ti to Cambridge, Massachusetts, impressing the citizenry along the route by firing off a mortar called Old Sow so the people might hear its deep roar. Here, too, appeared Benedict Arnold, who before his infamy had shared the command at Ticonderoga and led an attack on Burgoyne at Saratoga—or was it Freeman's Farm? Bemis Heights? Stillwater? And always through the narrative flashed the daring Ethan Allen and his Boys: outlaws, patriots, heroes. Why, I wondered, had Vermont been the "fourteenth state," not admitted into the Union until 1791?

Abruptly, to my astonishment, I had found the clue I was seeking: not the answer, but the Insoluble Problem itself.

WHERE WAS THE BATTLE OF SARATOGA FOUGHT? The story held all the familiar American ingredients—ambition, greed, real estate. It had begun a quarter of a century before the American Revolution, when Benning Wentworth, governor of the colony of New Hampshire, had decided to enlarge his reputation (hence Bennington) and his coffers by selling certain lands west of the Connecticut River to the aspiring settlers on the frontier. Which he did and continued to do for over a decade, despite the fact that the lands in question belonged to the colony of New York. Wentworth ignored such technicalities, as did the settlers of the region. But in 1764 the royal government in London upheld New York's claim to the land, thus invalidating all of Governor Wentworth's grants of property. Settlers on the "New Hampshire Grants," as the area was called, were obligated to repurchase their lands from New York.

Here emerged the notorious Green Mountain Boys. When the New York sheriffs came to call, the Boys built fortresses at such wonderfully named places as Otter Creek and Onion River, and commenced firing. Neighbors who accepted the Yorker jurisdiction might have a "birch seal" whipped into their naked backs. Fences were destroyed; cattle driven off; homes burned to the ground. Or, on happier occasions, the Boys might raise the roof from a cabin and replace it anew to signify conversion to the Yankee side.

Uncle Frank's Insoluble Problem, I realized at last, could be reduced to a honeycomb of constitutional law: Was "Saratoga" located in New Hampshire, New York, or Vermont? To answer the question would require a study of the colonial charters of the seventeenth century—the patents creating New Hampshire as a separate royal colony, the settlement made after the English conquest of New Netherland in 1664, and the Privy Council ruling of 1764 that found in favor of New York. After settling that jurisdictional dispute, it would also be necessary to consider the legal basis of Vermont's independence. Did Jefferson's Declaration of Independence—the idea that sovereignty derived from the consent of the governed—apply to the settlers of the Green Mountains? Did the people constitute an independent republic just because they said they did?

Upon this quagmire my career now hung—or so I feared.

Ethan Allen rescued me once again. In the historical documents of early Vermont I discovered that Allen and his brother Ira insisted that a secret charter, granted by King George III to a man named Philip Skene, had established an independent royal colony on the Grants prior to the outbreak of the Revolution. Such a charter would have justified the independence of Vermont both before July 4, 1776, and after. That would lay to rest the legal confusions of WHERE WAS THE BATTLE OF SARATOGA FOUGHT? But did the charter exist? And who was the mysterious Philip Skene?

The documents agreed about many essential points. Allen had indeed concocted a plan to create an independent colony, and he had found in Skene the ideal accomplice to implement it. Information about Skene was sketchy but persuasive. A retired military officer of the French and Indian War, he was master of two dozen Negro slaves, numerous servants, and 56,000 acres of choice Adirondack real estate that centered on a huge stone house at Skenesborough. Like many another British transplant, Major Skene expressed bold fantasies of empire. He saw himself as an aristocrat of the wilderness. Despite such pretensions, he got along with Allen, who once thanked Skene "for your generous & sotiable treatment to me at your house." Allen might not spell very well, but he had no trouble persuading Skene of "the honor and lucrative prospects" that would soon be his—if they could gain approval for a separate royal colony.

So Skene sailed for London in 1774, and soon reported his appointment as lieutenant governor of Crown Point and Ticonderoga; later, he was also made surveyor of the king's woods in the area. But then, as Ira Allen would write, "the calamity of an approaching war . . . put an end to the proposed negotiation." And this, most historians agreed, was the end of Skene's colony.

But if Skene's mission to London had failed, why had rumors of his colony persisted? Why had Ethan Allen secretly negotiated with the British to obtain copies of Skene's documents? Why had Ira Allen appealed for "a circumstantial account of Governor Skene's Charter?" Why was Skene depicted by patriot and Tory alike as "Governor?" (I found this appelation used by the Continental Congress in ordering his arrest!) Why, in fact, had such a distinguished group of delegates—John Hancock, John Adams, Silas Deane, Thomas Mifflin, and Christopher Gadsden, signers of the Declaration of Independence—personally greeted the arrival of Philip Skene's ship when it docked in Philadelphia in 1775? Why had they agreed to remain silent about the proceedings? And why had Skene (as he reluctantly confessed to this congressional delegation) thrown overboard certain papers "of consequence"?

The documentary record addressed these questions in the most teasing way. A representative from Pennsylvania to the Continental Congress said Skene was "Governor of Ticonderoga, Crown Point and the Lakes." But what area included the "Lakes"? John Adams reiterated the list in a letter to his wife, but added a tantalizing "etc." The Connecticut delegate declared that "Skene expected to have easy work [and] that he should soon get into his Kingdom at Crown Point." Was the word *kingdom* a metaphor of irony? Even the official minutes of the Congress added to the mystery. On June 8, 1775, the congressional *Journals* noted that Skene had been recently appointed governor of the forts at Ticonderoga and Crown Point, and that he claimed authority to raise a regiment in America; "from all this, apprehending that the said Skene *from his appointment* is a dangerous partizan of Administration." Why were the words "from his appointment" deliberately crossed out?

At this point my research had to stop. The answers to my questions—if there were answers—would require a journey to the British archives, something even Uncle Frank admitted was beyond the scope of his assignment. What impressed him most, however, was the invention of a new Insoluble Problem. WHERE WAS THE BATTLE OF SARATOGA FOUGHT? led in one direction, and I had gone off somewhere else. He would praise my scholarly resourcefulness, the prudent manipulation of evidence, and the urge, always, to take another step backward in time. That, he thought, was the essence of historical thinking. But I drew different conclusions from the experience: I emerged with a greater respect for the powers of instinct, the hunch, and the tenuous connections between the fantasies of one's boyhood and the sobriety of mature contemplation.

WHERE WAS THE BATTLE OF SARATOGA FOUGHT? was the first of many such curiosities that occupied my days for the next three years. "How sterile was Queen Mary's reign?" "How medieval was King James I?" "Whither the study of the War of 1812?" "Who fired the first shot at Fort Sumter?" Each topic would reveal a distinctive dilemma, a peculiarity of circumstance, and yet each demanded the same type of analysis and self-discipline. Gradually, the process of research wore away the brash edges; we no longer expected definitive conclusions. We came to realize— those few who survived in the program (Uncle Frank was right about that, too)—that historical scholarship was truly infinite: That every problem, if addressed properly, became an insoluble problem. And in that essential uncertainty lay the pull and the joy of a new fact.

SEVEN

City Limits

W ho said," Uncle Frank wanted to know, "that the Battle of Waterloo was won on the playing fields of Eton?" The *Oxford Dictionary of Quotations* tells the answer—and also an odd remark by one of the descendants of the duke of Wellington, claiming that the English general never uttered those words! (Thus are Insoluble Problems born and disseminated.) But if the moral of Uncle Frank's assignment was to suggest that the rigors of graduate school were intended to prepare us for the battlefields of historical scholarship, there was a distinct confusion between the self-discipline of Eton's athletes and what my friends and I preferred to do in our spare time, which was to drink.

There was no small irony in our preoccupation with alcohol. Our university town, as I said, was legally dry. But the bars on Chicago's Howard Street were friendly and convenient, and it was also possible to receive special home deliveries from the nearby suburbs. So on the weekends it was common for one of our ilk to buy an aluminum keg of beer, stow it in a garbage pail filled with ice cubes, and invite the entire history department to a party. Then we spent the evening making sure none of the beer went to waste. In one of her classier moments, Heather bought me an antique pewter mug, vintage George IV. Perhaps she hoped to keep me from becoming a total slob, but I don't think it worked.

The booze proved to be a great equalizer. Among the unquestioned verities of my era of graduate students was that when a professor started to drink, he simultaneously began to describe his Ph.D. oral examination. (Being dead sober, I shall forgo the details of mine.) The same, however, was true of those who hadn't yet experienced the ordeal. For the doctoral exams constituted the great traumatic ritual that separated professional from amateur, master from apprentice, and so loomed forever in our thoughts. The orals were the stuff of prudent terror and crazy nightmare. Everyone had a singular story: the friend who forgot his name, who forgot George Washington's name, who forgot the test altogether. And everyone could offer some personal confession, usually involving the breakdown of some bodily function.

There was sex at our parties, too, but it was always bent by the camraderie of drinking. The men generally congregated near the refrigerator, close to the supplies, while the wives and girlfriends' convened on the secondhand, motel-quality furniture in the living room. Seldom were these lines of gender breached, except by the few female graduate students who, by their very presence, defied academic convention. These women were certainly intelligent, but they were known less for their brains than for their aggressive, assertive style, their clamoring to be recognized and heard. In the mid-1960s the academic world did not consider such women a good investment. There were no women on the faculty; only one woman held a coveted fellowship. Nonetheless, these women graduate students, so much more vulnerable than we men, threatened our shaky egos. For the most part we avoided them—socially and sexually—and compensated by making nasty remarks about their various deficiencies. Sometimes a fledgling teaching assistant might bring a coed to our affairs, and usually she became the object of even viler remarks. Primarily we regaled ourselves with tales of impending doom, mimicked our mentors, or played at history trivia.

In this boozy atmosphere Heather and I thrived. New York Jews in the Midwest, we cultivated the image of iconoclasts. "Three generations of atheists," I'd boast whenever asked about my religious convictions. We drank too much, swore (at each other), and flaunted our sexuality. Heather especially delighted in embarrassing faculty wives with two lapel buttons she wore: LXIX and Tie Ethel's Tubes. We were also outspoken about our political dissent —hostile to the war and the draft, to Johnson, Humphrey, and Nixon alike. ("Vote for Johnson," said one of Heather's pins, "and get your Hump free.") That our bluntness offended the prevailing propriety, however, says more about our stodgy surroundings than any manifest radicalism. Our political views, like those of our student friends, remained incipient, a sort of background dissonance that bore little relationship to our daily lives. Whatever others thought of us, we were no more than good middle-class liberals.

Our posturing nonetheless brought some ironic consequences, particularly in shaping my career, which in those days was my exclusive concern. And it had to do, quite simply, with the most important decision a graduate student must face—choosing a dissertation topic. It would not only affect my progress toward the doctorate but would forever after define "my field"—MF—my area of expertise, the subject of my life's work, which jobs I would seek and obtain. In retrospect, my choice seems perfectly perverse and therefore perfectly consistent with my irreverent attitudes.

Given my upbringing and my philosophy of life, what could be more unnatural than choosing to specialize in Puritanism? But I did.

The Puritans, as we all know, wore those funny black hats and buckled boots, gave their children names like Increase, Prudence, and Mercy, and discoursed interminably, with dry intensity, about how the living soul could be prepared for divine ravishment. They were not, in short, the kind of people I was accustomed to befriending, and yet I lived in their company, shared their secrets, and learned their tongue for the two years it took to make my original contribution to "the advancement of learning," as we called the doctoral dissertation.

They proved, to my surprise, a lusty people, quite unlike the ordinary mortals who pass quietly through this world. The Puritans were dreamers, fighters, builders. Who else would envision and organize a veritable exodus three thousand miles from home to create in the wilderness a "city uppon a hill," as Governor John Winthrop so quaintly put it, and succeed?

Imagine the situation: the devil alive (among Puritans the terror is palpable), the power of the state an accomplice, good men clapped into dungeons, and all history compresses into an instant of decision. They see, far to the west, a sanctuary, "a shelter and a hiding place," and twenty thousand men, women, and children depart in fragile sailing ships to build Zion in a place called Massachusetts. But stop: In midpassage, as the gray Atlantic swells surround the tiny ship *Arbella*, Governor Winthrop stands at the mast and speaks. "Wee are a Company professing our selves fellow members in Christ," he says to his fellow passengers; "we ought to account our selves knitt together by this bond of love." He explains that Almighty God has given this particular people "a speciall Commission"—a task, a duty: "the eyes of all people are uppon us." If, despite all human frailty, they manage to create a godly community, declares Winthrop, "the Lord will . . . dwell among us."

Such grandiose dreams! Equivalent in our day to seeking utopia on the moon. And yet, like us, they were such pragmatists. Walk down any crooked street of Boston today and expect to meet the bearded Winthrop looking over your shoulder. Open the heavy doors of Old South Church, glance at the lofty dark-wood pulpit, and perceive instantly the power of the old Calvinist clergy. These Puritans linger in America not just as patriarchal symbols of a new nation but as the active ingredients, the yeast, of a distinct worldview that survives and permeates our postindustrial society.

What drew me to the Puritans (intellectually, at least) was a curiosity about beginnings, moments of creation. How did a distinctive American culture begin? How had Old World Europeans transplanted themselves and become new? (I never doubted then that they had.) And how, 350 years after the fact, could one observe the transformation, know it had occurred?

Here lay the essential insolubility: where to look for evidence. Surely the answer could be found in no single statement, no patriotic discourse that announced the arrival of a new, call it "American," sensibility. The history I wanted was interior. I was searching for a change of mind-sets, an evolution of conscious-ness, something that might not even exist. More than one pro-fessor advised me to find a more tangible subject—a biography, perhaps, or the collective portrait of a class of Harvard graduates. Their suggestions merely provoked my stubbornness. Besides, I believed that the history of ideas was indeed tangible, that the study of the past had to include the most human, if elusive, quali-ties: beliefs, passions, emotions. Otherwise, we might as well be writing the history of lions and tigers.

Intuition is not a demonstrable tool. But for years some lines of poetry had been rattling around my brain. (I have no idea where I first heard them.) The words seemed to offer a clue, a direction, for my research: "We were the land's before it was ours." How the Puritans interacted with the land, I surmised, might reveal how they viewed themselves as inhabitants here. We know that they rapidly altered the face of the land. Had the land altered them?

My initial presentation appeared straightforward. From the vantage of European history, the Puritans possessed various no-tions of America as a land of promise. It was, as Winthrop keenly appreciated, a refuge from troubles, a haven from oppression, a place to shelter the saving remnant no matter what happened in the Old World. To the Puritans, America also represented a land without evil, a vacant wilderness. (For reasons of theology and race, they did not worry about the prior claims of the native peoples.) On this place they could erect the new Israel. The writ-ings of exuberant explorers and real estate speculators contrib-uted optimistic images of a terrestrial paradise—a land of milk and honey waiting for those who would escape what Winthrop called the "fleshpots of Egypt" and cross the Red Sea of the seven-teenth century.

These were the expectations. How had they measured up to the reality?

The investigation nearly ended before it began. Among the mythic figures of American history writing looms the name Perry Miller. He remains the master scholar of Puritanism. The long-time Harvard professor had died the year before I enrolled in graduate school, a fact that exempted me from any personal failure in not having studied at his feet. But his massive studies of the Puritan mind dominated the field; no one could write about the Puritans without working through Miller. When I proposed my dissertation, therefore, I was told that it had already been done; Miller had written everything of consequence about Puritan intellectual history. (Later, I would learn that Miller had been told the same thing forty years earlier by his own mentors, which confirms my suspicion that while history may not repeat itself, historians certainly do.) But since Miller said very little about the natural environment—his assumption, rather, was that Puritan ideas transcended geography—my professors permitted me to proceed.

Thanks to Miller's enormous influence, the field of intellectual history had become rarified and abstract. First of all, he had argued that there existed such a thing as "the New England mind," an almost monolithic apparatus invented and defended by Puritan theologians, yet also understood and accepted by most ordinary people of the seventeenth century. At the center of this intellectual edifice stood the awesome God of Calvin; all other Puritan beliefs—about nature, society or politics—followed from that fundamental presence. Just to understand what he was talking about, I had to read the King James Bible from cover to cover, a purely intellectual exercise that scarcely dented my heathen soul. (But it did provide plenty of quotations to impress those friends who were far more pious but now, alas, less learned in the Scriptures.)

Miller claimed also to have scrutinized every single Puritan document of the seventeenth century; the publication of his references, he said, would equal the length of his enormous volumes. Such assertions (which recently have proved to be somewhat exaggerated) made the study of Puritanism both intimidating and defiant. It took a certain audacity—I am not bragging—to suggest that Miller, in his infinite wisdom, had failed to grapple with so elemental a topic as the American environment. And once I started my work, Miller seemed to hover above every idea, every quotation, reproving every fast generalization or wayward thought. I felt like that sculptor chiseling the Black Hills into presidential faces; somehow I would try to carve an original design.

Research is a lonely task: the eye playing with paper. At first, everything on a page seems potential evidence. You start by taking too many notes. But research is never passive; the facts don't speak for themselves. While the body sits and the light fades, the eye searches for patterns. From an infinite possibility of words and facts, the mind imposes order, logic, and significance. Early in my research, for example, I noticed that the colonists frequently discussed the presence of wolves in New England. By the seventeenth century, wild wolves had virtually disappeared from New England. So the wolves seemed to offer concrete evidence of the impact of the wilderness on the Puritan mind. What did it mean? Were the Puritans merely alarmed by the destruction of their cattle? Or was their preoccupation with wolves also a sign of their fear of the unknown environment? It was an intriguing problem: but, without more evidence, ultimately insoluble. Several dozen notes about New England wolves found their way into the discard pile.

My hunch about the wilderness nonetheless proved valid. Almost from the beginning of colonization, I found, Puritan leaders struggled to prevent the migration of settlers to more promising lands farther from the seacoast. Thus Governor Winthrop's ideal of a "city uppon a hill" conflicted with the obvious geographical opportunities of the west and also, apparently, with the expectations and desires of other good Puritans who preferred fertile acreage to a traditional social order. Yet habits of thought persisted. Despite the natural abundance of the New World, the Puritans did not see themselves as a people of plenty; I even found occasional evidence of a conservationist impulse. Nor did they envision a great future on the western frontier. Cotton Mather, the famous minister of Boston, described the west as the "back side" of settlement, which implied that the "front side" pointed east, toward the places from which they had come. Such insights, appropriately adorned by quotations from the Puritans, formed the basis of my dissertation.

The immense disparity between the Puritan world of the seven-

teenth century and that of a twentieth-century unbeliever created
problems of another sort. I became thoroughly bored with the
damned Puritans. I did not like the content of my work, the careful reading of theological disputations, sermons preached to the
converted, spiritual diaries, and business letters. Even less did
I like the accompanying perquisites: sitting in libraries, taking
notes, reading my way through three eyeglass prescriptions in
two years. I felt overwhelmed by the sheer number of words to be
read and written.

Other graduate students, feeling the same exhaustion, often
put aside their dissertations, delaying or, ultimately, abandoning
the hope of completion. Why did I persist? I liked being alone, I
think; the solitude was, as Winthrop would have put it, "a shelter and a hiding place." However tedious the act of research, it
protected me from having to consider the alternatives. And it
sheltered me from having to confront some personal facts of life
—the responsibilities, the intimacy, of what was proving to be
a rocky marriage. It was so much easier, surrounded by heaps
of notepaper and old books, to allow the momentum to sweep
me along.

One afternoon in January 1967, however, the snow began to fall
and continued falling. By the next morning, record-setting drifts
blocked our front door and buried the streets. All the momentum
stopped: The library was closed. Suddenly I was free from all the
seventeenth-century paraphernalia. I hadn't planned the holiday,
of course; but surely how I used the time could not have been
accidental. For instead of doing something different—or doing
nothing—I went directly to a book I had read once before, Erik
Erikson's masterpiece of psychohistory, *Young Man Luther*, and I
brought it into bed with me. The feeling was not unlike my adolescent scrutiny of Krafft-Ebing's *Psychopathia Sexualis:* I needed
some help.

Now the story of Martin Luther resonated with my own dilemma, accentuating the crisis, delineating my options. As Erikson explained it, Luther always felt destined to fulfill God's call
and yet also felt compelled to heed the more worldly demands of
his own father to undertake a practical career. Luther resolved

the crisis initially by avoiding it: He entered a monastery as a way of gaining time. In this way, said Erikson, Luther created a "moratorium"—a time away from crisis—from which he would later emerge with greater strength.

Despite all my delusions of grandeur, I never considered Martin Luther a role model; just the opposite, in fact. And this is what troubled me, darkened my thoughts. "It is probable," wrote Erikson, "that in all historical periods, some—and by no means the least gifted—young people do not survive their moratorium; they seek death or oblivion, or die in spirit." Here was the possibility I dreaded. For what was our life in graduate school in the 1960s if not monastic? Despite all the ferment of the decade, I scarcely had time to read the newspaper, much less join a cause or pursue some private interest. I was twenty-three, a married man, and I'd spent my entire life in school, nothing more. Had I sought this moratorium the better to find myself, only to be drowned by the minutiae of scholarship? The danger was not that I would flunk out and have to confront some unfriendly "real" world outside academia. The danger was that I would succeed marvelously—and "die in spirit."

When the snowplows opened the roads, nonetheless, I returned to the archives, feeling less confident and more confused. The best distractions I could find were those strange Puritan curiosities that appeared occasionally in the official records. I became engrossed, for example, in a legal case dating to the 1650s in the colony of New Haven: A young man had been accused of sodomizing his neighbor's sow. The evidence? A crop of piglets with an odd cast in their eyes, similar to the eyes of the accused. The authorities questioned the young man, and naturally, he denied any paternal responsibility. So the officials conferred again, reexamined the poor chap, and this time he confessed the deed. (Assuming his innocence and recognizing the absence of physical torture, one can only wonder at what obligations of obedience would compel such a confession. What does it suggest about loyalty to a political order, an ideology?) Upon hearing his confession, moreover, the court sentenced the man to death. At which point (the limits of his loyalty?) he retracted his confession. Whereupon he was again examined and brought to another confession. This time it stuck. One bright, sunny morning in Connecticut, the lad was hanged until dead—a warning to others. Theoretically, the sow had also defamed the name of God, but I found no evidence of a second execution. Perhaps the rights of property had intervened. In any case, when I recounted the case to a colleague, he topped it with one about a farmer who had saved the life of his sodomized mare by obtaining letters attesting to her previous virtue.

These barnyard affairs lightened my days, but never enough to compensate for a feeling of profound irrelevance. These were the 1960s, after all, an age of personal liberation, and I, the iconoclast, was locked into the seventeenth century. When I visited Boston in the springtime to examine some manuscript collections, the temptations to escape intensified. One morning I read the clinical details of Mistress Anne Hutchinson's miscarriage—"twenty seven lumps of man's seed, without any alteration, or mixture of any thing from the woman"—which Governor Winthrop considered ample proof of her heresy. That night I saw Michaelangelo Antonioni's *Blow Up,* the first mainstream movie with frontal nudity. I perused the chicken-scratched sermon notes of Master John Hull—the goldsmith of seventeenth-century Boston—while a nearby transistor radio blasted "What a Day for a Daydream," by the Lovin' Spoonful. I studied about King's Philip's War between Puritans and Narragansetts, and the Boston Red Sox headed for their first World Series in twenty some years.

The ultimate seduction was the daily-changing features at the Humphrey Bogart festival at a theater near Harvard Square. (The Bogey cult itself testified to an odd historical alienation: What did the wartime dilemmas of *Casablanca* mean to a generation of college students torn between going to Vietnam and marching on the Pentagon?) For me, Bogart was another link back to the forties, to that past just beyond my memory; I loved those black-and-white shadows of my parents' reality.

Each morning I arrived at the library determined to ignore the matinee show. By noon I would feel too restless to concentrate. As my mind wandered, I became aware of a long line of oil portraits that framed the manuscript reading room. Most were obviously eighteenth- or nineteenth-century gentlemen, scions of Harvard, no doubt, but one scholarly man clearly inhabited a modern business suit. His face attracted me. As I sat staring at him, debating a hasty bolt to the Bogart festival, he seemed to be telling me to stay. Usually, by three in the afternoon I didn't care what the old boy thought. But on my last day at this archive, I felt obligated to confront this curious man directly. As I approached his wall, I realized I'd been arguing with Professor Perry Miller.

The dissertation quickly became a book, and with its publication I would obtain my lifetime tenure at the University of Minnesota. I was only twenty-five, perhaps the youngest person to obtain tenure in the historical profession. In some ways it came too easily to me: I hadn't agonized enough to respect the milestone or appreciate its power against insecurity. So it's not without some embarrassment that I concede how limited my scholarly achievement now appears; I'd chiseled just another footnote at the pedestal of Professor Miller.

What soon threatened my security was totally unpredictable. In grappling with Miller's monolith of Puritanism, I had addressed the same types of questions he had asked: What is the relationship between ideas and society? How does the human mind respond to the dynamics of history? It had not occurred to me that these questions were themselves a function of history, were time-bound, and that Miller's preoccupation with what he called "the life of the mind" reflected the overriding concerns of his own generation: the grand ideological debates of the 1930s and 1940s. Perhaps I had been trapped by my emotional ties to that period. Whatever the reason, I had failed to see that a later generation of historians might prefer a different agenda. In any event, the newest writings about Puritanism blind-sided me.

While Perry Miller and his disciples had claimed the territory of intellectual history, a group of young historians (slightly older than me, actually, but positioned at the cutting edge of scholarship) began to publish books about the social history of colonial New England. They wrote about the history of the family, the evolution of town government, and patterns of landholding over the generations. Instead of examining the "mind" of New England, in other words, they focused on social behavior. Indeed, they said practically nothing about the issues raised by earlier intellectual historians. Yet precisely for this reason, their work was fresh and fascinating. They were introducing questions—about sexuality, marriage, child-rearing—that spoke to the major concerns of the late twentieth century, not to mention me personally.

I had missed the boat. While I had been confronting Miller's embattlements (and feeling as if I was banging my head against a stone wall), the social historians had staged a dramatic flank attack and carried the field. Perhaps my ignorance was the result of a midwestern, that is to say provincial, education; certainly I had been isolated from these newest trends of scholarship. So despite my personal success, I felt very much like Miller's Puritans, who migrated to New England to build a city on a hill and succeeded in the endeavor, only to discover too late that Puritanism in old England had advanced in another direction, leaving colonial Boston an artifact of old-fashioned values and London the center of the Enlightenment.

"If any actor," wrote Miller, "playing the leading role in the greatest dramatic spectacle of the century, were to attire himself and put on his make-up, rehearse his lines, take a deep breath, and stride onto the stage, only to find the theater dark and empty, no spotlight working, and himself entirely alone, he would feel as did New England around 1650 or 1660." Three hundred years later, I knew exactly what he meant.

EIGHT

To Find Another History

C lio is a jealous muse, and research is her weapon. Her demands are insatiable. For if historical knowledge depends on the careful amassing of documentation, rest assured: There is always something else, some additional fact somewhere to inspire a lifetime's quest. When I was in graduate school, rumors abounded about the search for the perfect footnote. One fellow in Wisconsin, we heard, had written a two-volume dissertation on the dairy industry in a single county during a ten-year period, "teat by teat."

Another doctoral candidate at a prestigious Ivy League university fashioned an intriguing alternative to the eternal quest. He made up the quotations he needed, and then invented archival "documents," which he footnoted. And not only did he manage in this way to obtain his Ph.D. but also a tenure-track job and the publication of the thesis as a book. Success, alas, did him in. For one of the specialists in his field happened to be working in the Library of Congress in the very collection cited in the phony footnotes when an advance copy of the book arrived for review. He was impressed by the cogent statements. But, try as he might, he could find the elusive sources not at all—and soon the entire fabrication came to light. The young professor lost his job; his Ph.D. was revoked. But one knowledgeable scholar pointed out that had the cheater actually done his homework, he would have found abundant evidence to support his conclusion.

Fraud was never in my heart. Only once did I knowingly invent a history—and that was purely for pedagogical purposes. I was teaching about the origins of the American Revolution and exploring the question of political conversion in the colonies, whereby dutiful subjects of King George became ardent supporters of General George Washington. How does a person loyal to one political system establish a commitment to a new leader, a new government?

As an example, I described Patrick Henry's famous speech in the Virginia House of Burgesses at the time of the Stamp Act crisis of 1765. "Tarquin and Caesar had each his Brutus," declared the fiery Henry; "Charles the First, his Cromwell; and George the Third. . . ." At which point, the shout "Treason! Treason!" echoed through the chamber. Henry paused until the clamor ceased and then continued, ". . . George the Third may profit from their example. If this be treason, make the most of it."

Henry's patriotic splendor derived from a long history of radical politics in the colonies, but I suggested that an important component of his political development lay in the very process of speaking. The rhetoric of revolution had its own momentum; words, once articulated, could not be withdrawn. The logic of his language could not be denied or ignored. In Henry's case, the speech of 1765 made his later statements seem both plausible and imperative: "If this be treason" led logically to "Give me liberty or give me death." By then, the spoken word had eliminated any third alternatives.

This lecture on language and political commitment formed the core of my midterm examination, which I graded on the basis of the students' familiarity with the ideas of the American Revolution and their ability to explain the relationship between words and actions. And, as happens with most good exams, the grades revealed a healthy diversity. Later, in discussing the test, I reiterated the case of Patrick Henry: By 1776 his speeches had boxed him into a corner. Political rhetoric, I suggested, was not simply a rationalization of one's economic self-interests, something "made up" to justify more "real" motives, but it had a reality of its own.

After the midterm, the course proceeded through the American Revolution, the Constitution, and the new nation unto the Era of Good Feelings. At this point I introduced the problem of how Americans of the early nineteenth century struggled self-consciously to create a national culture. As a "new nation," with thirteen diverse origins, the United States lacked a common heritage of heroes and symbols, the attachments that bind citizens to a people's government. But in the aftermath of the War of 1812, a few popular writers attempted to fill the void by inventing an appropriately patriotic American history. They did not always stick to the facts, however, and instead strove to give the American people good heroes with whom to identify. Among these myth-makers was a Virginian named William Wirt, who in 1817 published a book entitled *Sketches of the Life and Character of Patrick Henry*. In order to make his subject an exemplary figure, Wirt sometimes invented his own version of American history. In fact, it was Wirt—not Patrick Henry—who first said, "If this be treason, make the most of it."

The lecture I had given some weeks earlier on the causes of the American Revolution—the class that had shaped the midterm examination and the students' grades—had been based, I now confessed, on a lie. Although Patrick Henry had given a speech similar to the one quoted in Wirt's biography, he had responded to the cry "Treason!" in a much humbler, conciliatory way. According to the only firsthand account of Henry's speech of 1765, he had apologized for any offense and said "he would show his loyalty to his majesty King George the third, at the expense of his last drop of blood, but what he had said must be attributed to the interest of his country's dying liberty . . . and the heat of passion might have led him to have said something more than he intended." Henry begged for pardon, at which point the other members of the House of Burgesses rose to their feet to support him, "on which that affair was dropped." While Henry did say (a decade later) "Give me liberty . . ." that statement obviously could not be related to an earlier speech, "If this be treason . . ." because he never said it!

The students were outraged, particularly those who hadn't done too well on the midterm. I didn't care. My deception gave them what I considered three important lessons: First, that although Patrick Henry might have been a poor example, language and rhetoric do exist in history—and not merely as the superstructure of reality but at its foundations. What people think, what they say they think, is psychologically real. Lesson two, that the creation of American nationalism in the 1800s was not "natural" but the result of deliberate mythological invention. ("Mythology," one of my history professors used to say, "is the history we do not believe; history is the mythology we do believe.") And the third lesson: that students should never believe their professors at face value.

Among scholars there is an axiom that you never really understand a subject until you've taught it. Teaching history drastically altered my sense of the American past. And I believe that what happened to me was not untypical of my generation. Instead of changing the facts of American history, we discovered a history that the old facts could not explain. We did not invent new facts, either; they had always existed. But, through education, we had been trained not to see them, for they contradicted the assumptions that most historians held. And what brought these facts into the sunshine was not some superior wisdom; it was the political crisis of the late 1960s.

The revelations began for me in 1968. One month after the assassination of Martin Luther King, I started my first teaching job in Chicago, a city on the verge of revolution. Rioting there after the King assassination had provoked Mayor Daley to issue "shoot to kill" orders to the police, who, even in normal times, were not famous for their restraint. Ordinary politics wore a personal edge. I recall the haggard expression of a young, dark-eyed student wearing an "I Like Bobby" button as she wrote my final examination about the Constitution on the day the candidate lingered between life and death in a Los Angeles hospital. That summer, street protests against the Democratic National Convention produced the infamous "police riot." In the fall my students divided about evenly between inner-city blacks, justly suspicious of any white authority figures, and working-class whites deeply antagonistic to the civil rights movement and the demand for black power. Several of my students had been arrested for antiwar activity. One clean-cut fellow was serving time in jail each weekend, upon the condition that he remain in classes from Monday to Friday.

It was a peculiar setting in which to launch a teaching career. My education had not prepared me for the needs of my students. Just a few years before, the idea of Afro-American history conjured up images of Tarzan and bongo drums. As I first learned the subject, the history of Negroes began with the institution of slavery, which, despite occasional abuses by psychotic whites, had served to transmit the values of civilization to a savage race. By the time I began to teach my own classes, these stereotypes had been muted: The history of Negroes did indeed appear to be unfortunate, but there was still an undeniable progress from barbarism to civilization. (Such attitudes, by the way, were often held by blacks; as recently as the 1970s, this idealization of black progress infused Alex Haley's *Roots*, which may explain its enormous popularity.) Despite my Ph.D. degree, I had acquired no education about black history. But I did know something about Freud.

When I presented my first lecture about slavery, therefore, I speculated about the psychology of racism. Why was it, I asked, that white people disliked the natives of Africa? Why did the Europeans consider them inferior beings? Was it the bestiality of their surroundings? As I spoke, the white kids from Cicero and Berwyn, ethnic suburbs that had greeted Martin Luther King with curses and bricks, began to snicker and hoot. Were Africans regarded as children of the jungle because Europeans thought they slept with apes and gorillas? The snickers exploded with laughter; the blacks, meanwhile, glared angrily. Is that why blacks have been considered supersexed? Is that why whites have paid so much attention to the size of black genitals? Now the whistles came from the other side.

And what about the color black? Black was traditionally viewed as evil, wicked, dirty, bad; white represented purity, cleanliness, good. Where did those images come from? More to the point— here was my Freudian coup—black people really weren't black at all. The students looked at each other furtively. They were brown, of course. And what other everyday object—bodily object—was also brown? And wasn't there a racial stereotype that said brown people smelled funny?

Total silence. No one had heard such things before. I was suddenly very afraid, physically afraid. There was no escape. Standing alone at the bottom of the lecture hall (being paid to stand there), I could only finish the job. Yet the shock of my questions had tamed the classroom. I went on to give a lucid, if debatable, analysis of race prejudice. I was lucky to get off so easily. What disturbed me, though, was how much I had to rely on my wits rather than my education. I was really quite ignorant.

Like most historians who responded to the political crisis of the 1960s, I eventually acquired some proficiency in black history. Instead of limiting my lectures to the evils of American slavery— which was, after all, a white-made institution—we explored other dimensions of black experience: the nature of Afro-American religion, the structure of the black family, styles of political resistance, and the conflict between racial integration and the desire for a black community. The shift in focus was easily absorbed into the traditional history courses; and so most undergraduates of the 1980s can learn more about black history, if they wish, than most senior professors knew just half a generation ago.

The implications of this "new" history are impressive. Take, for example, the story of the conquest of smallpox. As told in the conventional (white) history, it was the story of Progress—one generation of scientists benefiting from the knowledge of their predecessors until, around 1776, Dr. Edward Jenner invented a vaccination procedure in London. In this saga of progress, one usually finds a short digression about a smallpox epidemic in Boston, Massachusetts, in 1721. At that time the traditional remedy for smallpox was prayer. Whole towns might close down for a day of fast, hoping that communal repentance would persuade the Lord to mitigate His wrath. But in 1721 a few ministers of Boston, led by the celebrated Cotton Mather, introduced the idea of inoculation as an effective preventative practice. The New England medical profession, then as now conservative to the quick, fought against the scheme. But a single physician, Zabdiel Boylston, broke ranks and agreed to experiment with inoculation. He probably saved hundreds of lives. In this way American medicine takes its place in the story of scientific progress.

But how had Cotton Mather heard of inoculation? There are two extremely revealing passages in Mather's writings that touch on this question. The first is a diary entry dated December 15, 1706: "Some gentlemen of our Church, understanding . . . that I wanted a good Servant at the expense of between forty and fifty Pounds, purchased for me, a very likely Slave, a young Man, who is a Negro of a promising Aspect and Temper, and this Day they presented him unto me. I putt upon him the Name of Onesimus."

The second relevant text appears in a letter sent by Mather to the Royal Society of London and dated July 12, 1716:

> . . . ye Method of Inoculation, I had from a Servant of my own, an Account of its being practiced in Africa. Enquiring of my Negro-Man Onesimus, who is a pretty Intelligent Fellow, Whether he ever had ye Small-Pox, he answered Yes and No; and then told me that he had undergone an Operation, which had given him something of ye Small-Pox, and would forever preserve him from it, adding, That it was often used among ye Guaramantese, and whoever had yet Courage to use it, was forever free from ye Fear of the Contagion. He described ye Operation to me, and showed me in his Arm ye Scar. . . .

From these extracts we may draw some conclusions. Black people, obviously, were not invisible in colonial New England, and their status there seems similar to that of blacks in the southern colonies. Whatever the origins of race prejudice, geography and climate were probably of small significance. Equally obvious was that blacks in colonial America, however they were renamed by their masters, retained the basic cultural identity of their antecedents. In explaining inoculation to Cotton Mather, Onesimus could draw upon centuries of African (and Arab) tradition. That the Reverend Cotton Mather listened to Onesimus —and, indeed, learned much from him—also testifies to a type of cultural change quite different from the notion of Progress. For certainly the idea of inoculation was brought to eighteenth-century Boston not through the natural development of scientific learning but by an abrupt cultural contact with the outside world. In other words, it was a historical *discontinuity* that made the difference.

My belated discovery of such examples of black history revealed the serious deficiencies of my advanced education, but not until I moved to Minnesota in 1969 did I confront a minority group whose history would change my entire understanding of the American past, and with it, my career. In Minneapolis I encountered for the first time American Indians, who, like the majority of blacks in Chicago, lived in great poverty. A very few managed to go to college, and these students introduced me to a historical world I never knew existed. Like most New Yorkers, my previous acquaintance with American Indians could be reduced to the names of summer camps in the Catskill Mountains and the poker-faced shield on my neighbor's Pontiac. When I met real American Indians, I confronted questions I had never before considered.

Who, for example, was Pontiac? No friend of the white people! He was a leader of the Ottawa tribe, which lived near the Great Lakes at the time of the French and Indian Wars (1754–63). He was also a disciple of a prophet named Neolin, a Delaware Indian who traveled through the Ohio River valley preaching that the native tribes must resist Western civilization and return to their traditional way of life. "Wherefore do you suffer the whites to dwell upon your lands?" Neolin asked. "Drive them away; wage war against them."

Thus inspired, Pontiac attacked British and American bases along the western frontier in 1763. He personally led the siege against Fort Detroit (which makes naming an automobile after him somewhat ironic, though not as peculiar as naming a great Indian marathon runner Silver Cloud after a model of the Rolls Royce; that happened in the 1920s!) Pontiac's uprising drove terror through the colonial settlements and contributed to a growing suspicion among American colonists that the royal government was not serving their interests. Meanwhile, the government in London responded to Pontiac's war with the Proclamation Act of 1763, which forbade further settlement of the western lands— another grievance to the land-hungry colonists—and dispatched redcoats to America, which added to the costs (and taxes) that the colonists were expected to pay. Lacking the technology to wage war, however, Pontiac's uprising soon dwindled in military significance, though the chief continued to fight for another two years. His brief appearance on the historical stage serves now as a symbol of the coming imperial conflict between Britain and her colonies. Yet in another sense, Pontiac illuminates a dark side of the American war for independence. For in claiming rights to the western territories, Americans no less than the British treated North America as an empty continent—devoid of civilization and human beings, as they defined them.

For me, the shock came in discovering just how many of these "nonhumans" existed. Statistics in the age before computers can hardly be considered an exact science, and population estimates were often based on nothing more than the wishful thinking of some colonial real estate promoter. But even allowing for a 100 percent margin of error, the size of the native population was immense. As historians, anthropologists, and archeologists reconstruct the evidence, it appears that there were perhaps as many as 50 million people living in the Western Hemisphere at the time of Columbus's first voyage in 1492. Of these, perhaps 5 million lived in what is now the United States. (The standard textbook estimate of the 1960s, by contrast, was 100,000.) Fifteenth-century Huron villages around what is now Detroit may have been as densely populated as London and Paris at that time. By no reasonable accounting can North America be considered a virgin wilderness awaiting the arrival of civilization.

Equally shocking was the fate of these people. Of the estimated 8 million people who inhabited the Caribbean islands in 1492, virtually no descendants survived in 1600. The destruction of Aztec and Inca societies by the Spanish conquistadores can be compared to the Jewish Holocaust of the twentieth century. When the Puritans landed in Massachusetts in the early seventeenth century, they found piles of human bones that testified to a terrible mass death. To them, the tragedy demonstrated divine will (and the Puritans promptly claimed the unoccupied lands for themselves). Today, historians believe the mortality resulted from the introduction of European diseases, especially smallpox, for which the Indian people lacked immunity. And these epidemics were only part of a larger assault on the ecological balance—the indiscriminate killing of wildlife, the importation of new plants, the erosion of the soil. Such consequences may not have been deliberate, but we should not forget the demographic effects of sheer cruelty, enslavement, and wars of conquest that *intended* to exterminate the Indian tribes.

The stark facts of American Indian history, like those of black history, completely overturned my understanding, my assumptions, about the central themes of American history. The idea of the "city upon a hill," for example, and the notion that the United States was, as Lincoln put it, "the last, best hope of earth" —to use two ubiquitous quotations—suggest that the American people had carried human culture to a pinnacle of achievement. As the historian of such a people, I expected to share in their progress, and perhaps even to use my knowledge of the glorious past to enliven opportunities for the future. Among my generation of graduate students, historian Arthur M. Schlesinger, Jr., President Kennedy's special adviser, stood as an important symbol of how influential a good historian could become.

The perspective of the American Indians shattered those illusions. The exodus of Europeans to America was no repetition of the Israelites leaving the fleshpots of Egypt, as the Puritan Winthrop claimed, but simply the military conquest of one people by another. Moreover, the origins of American history would not be found in the world of Ferdinand and Isabella or Sir Walter Raleigh, nor among the West Africans carried across the Atlantic in chains, but among the indigenous peoples who had first populated the New World thirty thousand years before the life of Christ. To see American history from the perspective of American Indians was like running a movie in reverse. As the chronology fled backward, the plot became clearer, more blatant; the progressive narrative appeared false, self-serving, even evil.

One day in Minnesota, a student dressed like a hippie came into my office with a copy of a book he said I should read. It contained the autobiographical reminiscences of an Oglala Sioux holy man, published under the title *Black Elk Speaks*. "I am going to tell you the story of my life," the old man began; "and if it were only the story of my life I think I would not tell it; for what is one man? . . . So many other men have lived and shall live that story, to be grass upon the hills." Here was an ultimate rejection of white history—not just the narrative of American nationalism that glorified westward expansion but an attack on secular history itself. For Black Elk recognized that narrative history, with its celebration of individual heroes, was an expression of modern values and thus another instrument of his people's oppression.

Black Elk was a prophet to his people, and he offered them a sacred vision that promised to restore their power as a viable nation. He was also, however, a survivor of the massacre at Wounded Knee in 1890, and he knew that the spiritual power of the red people could not match the force of Springfield rifles and Gatling guns. "When I look back now from this high hill of my old age," he said, "I can still see the butchered women and children lying heaped and scattered all along the crooked gulch. . . . And I can see that something else died there in the bloody mud, and was buried in the blizzard. A people's dream died there."

As I read these words I realized how much my own dreams had died. I had become involved in American history because it promised resurrection. It gave me the power to create the past; I could restore life to people who had disappeared long ago. In entering the historical profession, however, I had joined an academic orthodoxy that defined American history from the perspective of the prevailing leadership. I no longer believed in that history. But what was I to do? I could switch sides and battle from within the institution—or I could step outside.

To call my belated awakening a crisis of faith may sound crudely spiritual, and yet, after all, that is exactly what it was. That Christmas, one of my students presented me with a sampler of Americana, and she inscribed it, "always remember that your knowledge belongs to the people." Romantic idealism? It was just the push I needed. Within the year I was prepared to bid farewell to academia. "It may be," said Black Elk in conclusion, "that some little root of the sacred tree still lives. Nourish it then, that it may leaf and bloom and fill with singing birds." I chose those words as the epigraph for my first nonacademic book.

NINE

Young Turks

I nside the walls of academia—and outside, too—History was my world. I had become supremely literate; in less than eight years I had catapulted from high-school mediocrity to a tenured professorship. I loved to go to my classes with a bundle of Insoluble Problems—Who was George Washington? How do you know?—just to make otherwise lethargic students angry and force them to look again at the platitudes they had imbibed. But even more I loved the solitude of research. At one time I had three private offices—one in the library, one in the history department, and one at home—and in these shells I spent my life. As a student, such intensity could be accepted, rationalized away, even lauded by the unmovable "requirements" of the curriculum and by the belief that one day it would end. I was as surprised as my wife when it did not end. Because I desired this cloistered life. Which is not to say that I was happy.

My discontents were not exactly personal. The "tumultuous sixties" were nearly over before their spirit intruded into my consciousness. Although I was mildly aware of the political turmoil —civil rights and black power, Vietnam and the draft—the issues seemed to have little to do with my life, my career, and my interests, and so were easily submerged by a sunny, liberal optimism. In a curious reversal of generations, it was my father who first challenged my complaisance in the mid-1960s. I had just returned from a visit to the local draft board, where I was assured by the middle-aged clerk that I had nothing to fear. "We have a large pool," she said; by which she referred to the blacks and Puerto Ricans from the nearby projects and the many sons of blue-collar workers whose occupations would never qualify for a deferment. They stood between Vietnam and me. It was one of the ironies of my family's politics, the decision made in the golden age of suburbia to live among people of color.

"Hey, historian," my father accosted me in a voice laden with sarcasm. "When is this Vietnam going to end?" He pronounced Vietnam with a French accent.

I offered the liberal response: politics was personalities. The Kennedys were one kind of animal; Lyndon Johnson quite another. The president could not afford to back down on Vietnam. It would look bad, weaken the country's reputation. Besides, he was too much a Texan to retreat; the Alamo and all that. With another personality, say a shift in administrations, the war would soon end.

What I remember most vividly is the smirk on my father's face. He was half-smiling, a familiar glint in his dark eyes that I read as a smug tolerance for his son's degeneracy. Nothing hostile, but no respect, either. "Do you really believe it's that simple?" he asked at last.

I rambled on about Johnson's commitment, his ensnarement in the language of anticommunism.

Who, my father wanted to know, was getting rich off the war? Shades of the Old Left. I was appalled, annoyed by his logic. "You don't think Johnson is part of some Wall Street conspiracy, do you?" I replied angrily, preparing for one of those marathon fights that seemed to go on whenever I discussed the war with people of his generation.

He did not respond, which gave the impression that I had won the point. We let the matter drop. Neither of us wished to spoil the pleasure of our rare late-night talks when I was back in New York. But if my thinking about Vietnam did not change, his line of argument played in my mind. I did not believe that corporations caused the Vietnam War, but I was surprised that he did. It was so easy to dismiss the Wall Street conspiracy as unenlightened anachronism. What did it mean that he still espoused a Marxist theory of class warfare? But my doubts, such as they were, had nothing to do with my work, and I was content to live among Green Mountain Boys and Puritans.

Not until my formal schooling ended did I open myself to questions of contemporary history. Perhaps I needed security—economic, professional, personal—to do so. In any case, as a faculty member, the issues raised by Vietnam were inescapable. My students looked to me for answers, raising the embarrassing word (ugly to conservatives) *relevance* in relation to their education. It was not enough to know about the past. I was also responsible for interpreting it to people living in the present. And how I chose to present the subject had obvious political and moral consequences. I recall the difficulty of teaching about colonial politics —the habits of deference that permitted self-perpetuating oligarchies to govern the society—until, to my delight, I realized the obvious analogy to Mayor Daley's Chicago machine, with which my students were intimately familiar. Following the precedent of colonial yeomen, who often could discern no difference among political candidates, many of my students announced they would not vote in 1968. For the same reasons, neither did I. Similarly, my lectures on Manifest Destiny, the enduring spirit of the "city uppon a hill," led inevitably to the American presence in Southeast Asia. In such discussions history could never be neutral. For the first time I had to abandon my academic innocence and take a stand.

The politicized atmosphere among students continued to percolate upward. Those who believe that the 1960s were a radical decade—as distinguished from the sleepy 1970s—fail to appreciate the belated conversion of liberals like me. Indeed, the radical Students for a Democratic Society had virtually fizzled out of existence before we erstwhile liberals formed a critical mass against the war. Yet given my liberal sympathies, it was eminently reasonable to cancel classes during the Moratorium Day protests in the autumn of 1969 and then to parade publicly to the nearest federal building, where the poet John Berryman addressed a large crowd about the indignities of the war. I made it a point to wear a white shirt and a tie to show that the march was respectable. Other demonstrations followed, each a little more frustrated at the indifference inside the White House, each a little more hostile to the power of government. Not without cause. For raising his voice, one student friend was plugged in the stomach with a billy club; a woman I knew was beaten across the knees by the campus police. By the following spring it was not hard to identify with the four students murdered at Kent State in Ohio.

During the ensuing student strike, I met my classes at night in a shabby off-campus apartment. The students were sophomores, eighteen or nineteen years old; I was twenty-six, the age of an older brother. The setting inspired a self-conscious sense of experimentation. Sitting on pillows scattered around the floor, we felt an urgency to understand this abrupt collapse of normal institutions; critical education seemed more important than ever before. It was now appropriate, imperative, to move beyond the familiar rhetoric of American history—the story of progress, democracy, and beneficent technology—to confront the origins of the current crisis. For the first time as a historian I had to grapple with questions of power: Who ruled the country and for what purpose? And at the moment I spoke the word *class*—meaning an economically related group that wields power—I saw that smirk on my father's face. The term no longer seemed an anachronism. "Up the ass to the ruling class," was the oft-repeated student cry; "power to the people!"

Such rhetorical excess assumed a personal shape that summer when one of the students from my unofficial classroom was arrested along with seven coconspirators for attempting to destroy draft board records. The original charge was "sabotage"—a word that derives from the French *sabot,* the wooden shoe worn by early factory workers that proved to be an effective weapon against unfriendly industrial machinery. The relationship between class warfare and Vietnam thus seemed apparent. Perhaps for this reason, the government changed the indictments to a more familiar conspiracy to violate the Selective Service Act. By then, the "Minnesota 8" were defending themselves not on Marxist dialectics but on grounds of "higher allegiance"—the doctrine that there are moral laws higher than congressional statutes that command one's loyalty.

It was an argument old as the republic and, because of my expertise in American history, I was asked to attend some student forums, serving as a faculty prop to lend respectability to the discussions. The obvious historical analogy I proposed related to the abolitionist movement of the last century. Determined to overthrow the "peculiar institution" of slavery, William Lloyd Garrison had once burned the Constitution on a public stage, while William H. Seward, destined to become Lincoln's secretary of state, announced on the Senate floor that there existed a "higher law" than the Constitution, which justified illegal actions. Their moral outrage, I explained, brought attendant risks: Garrison was once paraded through the streets of Boston with a rope around his neck; other abolitionists were tarred and feathered, even killed. The tradition of dissent, I suggested, was clear. But while my appeals to history may have contributed to the self-righteous climate that infused the antiwar movement, they proved of little help to the local defendants. The Minnesota 8 were tried, convicted, and sent away to do time.

The comparison to the abolitionists, however, reflected more than historical precedent. They were, of course, the vanguard of the larger society. Abolitionist ideas, formalized in the Thirteenth Amendment, became one of the accepted bulwarks of freedom in the twentieth century. In risking their lives, moreover, the abolitionists had demonstrated the importance of vicarious suffering. Northern whites of the nineteenth century might be indifferent to the troubles of little black Sambo, but attacks on the liberty of white men, such as Garrison, showed the inherent danger of southern slavery; the "peculiar institution" was threatening the freedom of white men. One hundred years later, attacks on civil rights workers, many of them northern whites (including a classmate of mine from Queens who was killed in Mississippi), would testify to the continuing danger of racial injustice, gain converts to the freedom movement in the north, and accelerate passage of civil rights legislation in the 1960s. As in the nineteenth century, those victims had attained an honored status among liberals and radicals alike. In admiring their conviction, their courage, I felt no small embarrassment at having spent the 1960s on the sidelines.

The sacrifice of students to Vietnam—both draftees and resisters—now symbolized a similar menace. Bad enough that young lives were interrupted and wasted (a word that in Vietnam meant killed). Such bitter realities provided a moral imperative. But the war also threatened the freedom of dissenters. Nearly everyone I knew in the antiwar movement believed his telephone was tapped; in fact, many were. My closest colleague, we later learned, was under FBI surveillance. And because the federal government was the main architect of the war and the feared repression, a strident antiauthoritarian politics pervaded campus life. In this way old forms of loyalty to flag and country withered. The unconscious glue that held the society together, the delicate threads that in normal times assure one's allegiance, were coming apart, perhaps forever. One did not have to read Marx to know about alienation or to dream of a revolution. Ordinary, otherwise law-abiding citizens had become political outsiders, if not enemies of the state.

Except that none of us was alone. The politicization of the university stimulated a remarkable camraderie among students and younger faculty, most of whom had spent the sixties quietly at work in graduate school. Having been passive observers of student unrest and administrative insensitivity, we were prepared to embrace a variety of issues concerning academic power and reform. Student representation on university committees was one early campaign; the search for minority graduate students another. These issues provoked angry debates between conservatives dedicated to preserving the values of "in loco parentis" and a new breed of Young Turks who identified with the demands of their students. Having waged such battles as a college student (and now possessing tenure), I gladly joined the fray.

The struggles became more heated when addressing matters of curriculum. In a typical "liberal" reform, the university mandated raising the value of all course credits from three to four, a 33 percent inflation policy that meant that students took fewer courses, faculty taught fewer courses, and the administration hired fewer employees. Elected director of undergraduate studies (in itself a radical "coup"), I had to supervise an overhaul of all course requirements. The questions involved were profound, focusing ultimately on the role of history in a democratic society. What, we were asking, was an educated electorate supposed to know about the past? Yet the debates typically reflected the self-interests of specific constituencies. While conservatives suggested continuing traditional liberal arts requirements and a mere juggling of credit numbers to accommodate the inflation, the Young Turks proposed that students be forced to study the history of non-Western societies. An enlightened youth, so the thinking went, would avoid the ignorance that had led the country into Vietnam. But although that goal was admirable, curriculum reforms would reduce enrollments in such traditional courses as ancient and medieval history and so would imperil several established fiefdoms. (To college administrators, enrollment remained the bottom line of academic efficiency.) The traditionalists demanded due respect for the classic Western education. That such arguments persist twenty years later underscores their essential insolubility. In the short run, we forged uneasy compromises and came to expect a chronic polarization within the department.

I dwell on these feuds precisely because of their "academic" nature. Perhaps it is the relative powerlessness of college professors—the inverse relationship between their erudition and the ability to influence public policy—that explains the intensity of professorial strife. In a realm of small rewards, every morsel has its distinctive value. Each year, for example, we submitted formal "brag sheets" listing our recent attainments—publications, committee assignments, student advisees, university service; these were tallied, compared, judged, rewarded. Cliques evolved; bickering ensued. Grown men quarreled about sums equivalent to a couple of six-packs a week!

What threw these animosities into perspective was the sudden death of our chairman, a middle-aged medievalist with considerable skill and influence in university affairs. At midcareer he had put aside his historical research to become an extremely efficient administrator. His death touched me deeply. As I saw his coffin lowered into the frozen Minnesota earth on the coldest, grayest day in my life, I struggled to comprehend his legacy. Amid the dull academic eulogies, I could see that the institution, to which he had rendered the last years of devotion, would go on as before. Already we had elected his successor. But how else could an institution respond? What did it matter to the institution that, in order to serve it, he had abandoned his first love, History? I shivered uncontrollably. For I had glimpsed the emptiness of his sacrifice, and I vowed at his gravesite never to confuse History with history departments.

The limits of academic achievement contrasted with a fresh, irreverent lifestyle sprouting around the campus. One of the Young Turks handed me a marijuana-laced cigarette, and the world never looked quite the same again. On strictly legal grounds we were guilty of felony crimes, which both whetted our paranoia about Big Brother and reinforced our contempt for authority. After all, we could get twenty years in the slammer for sheer enjoyment! Pot smoking, in this light, proved a force for liberation; it provided a distinctively woozy, ironic perspective about the most mundane activities. Drug fiends, in my memory, were forever laughing at the seriousness and pretension of the sane and sober. Euphoria also induced a peculiar creativity—for example, elaborate schemes and plans to get really rich and never have to work again—which by morning had evaporated. Nonetheless, this obsessive interest in escape reflected a real fear of inertia. I started to write a novel, many novels, in fact, which were on second reading remarkably awful. They revealed less about my talent, however, than a craving for expression, the desire to hear myself speak in another voice, and the discovery that maybe I could.

In this ambience of innovation I stopped wearing ties and jackets, let my hair grow, and cultivated a broad red mustache with matching muttonchops—all part of the trendy rebellion against looking adult. Our students became models of sartorial splendor. Around the time of Earth Day (April 30, 1970), a moment to reflect on the woeful condition of the environment, it became fashionable to seek a more natural, self-reliant style. I learned to make candles and tie-dye shirts, bought whole-grain breads at the food co-ops, and walked around barefoot, even to class. The idea of "living lightly" on the earth appealed to middle-class dissidents searching for an alternative to the prevailing capitalist, bureaucratic values. Lacking any hope of changing the economic or political system, we endeavored to be less dependent on its wealth and expectations. I described myself as a "friendly anarchist."

And what could be more friendly than falling in love?

Blame it on the long Minnesota winters or the Beatles promising "here comes the sun" or maybe the aromatic grass that aroused one's hedonism. As I approached my thirtieth birthday, the craving for maturity that had rushed me into marriage in the early 1960s had become suspect. A stronger relationship might have withstood such pressures. But mine had always been volatile and tenuous. On the very day I submitted my finished dissertation, I had gone off with a woman, discovered a fabulous tenderness, and just as quickly succumbed to a paralyzing guilt that lasted even after I ended the affair. Responsibility prevailed. My wife and I had a child. When he was newborn, I cradled his delicate head in my arms and studied my future. I wept in joy and awe. Some day, I knew, he would bury me.

This certainty—no doubt the prideful illusion of patriarchy—accentuated my feeling of stability but also brought a terrifying mood of entrapment, claustrophobia. I grappled with my conscience, fell in love, fell out of love. I saw clearly that my marriage could well endure into the twenty-first century—or it could end thirty years sooner. Increasingly, the choice seemed arbitrary. During the late 1960s and early 1970s, an epidemic of divorce swept through academia, particularly among young historians, adding grist to the national trend of divorces that so alarmed my mother. These were not baby boomers (or latter-day Yuppies) raised under the permissive dictates of Doctor Benjamin Spock; nor were they glib narcissists (as described by Christopher Lasch) who could not see beyond the pleasure principle. They were respectable people, friends and colleagues and students, and each phone call to help someone move his boxes of books into a new homestead lent legitimacy to my own frustrations and desires.

I stood, finally, on a bridge above the Mississippi River—the very bridge from which John Berryman had leaped to his death the previous year—and stared at the snowy countryside as the gray waters swept past the bare trees and around a gentle bend. Here was one way to answer the riddle. But then I became aware of a young man standing next to me, studying the same stark landscape. I did not see his face. But apparently we stood together long enough, unmoving, unspeaking, to reach the same conclusion. I laughed aloud. Whatever the fantasy or the despair, it was just too damn cold to live or die at that spot. Slightly out of stride, we both walked off the bridge toward the late afternoon sun. Later, after I told the strange story to my wife, we became another divorce statistic.

TEN

The Other Boswell

My dilemma was deeply personal but not unique. By the early 1970s a new breed of historian had emerged. Influenced by the multitude of social and political issues of the 1960s—the civil rights movement, Vietnam, the sexual revolution and the beginnings of women's liberation, the anti-authoritarianism of the youth culture—scholars and students were asking new questions of the past, seeking new kinds of information, and so challenging the accepted values about what was important in history. Such ferment stimulated innovation. As the content of history shifted toward new subjects, historians opted for new methodologies: demography, cliometry, comparative history, psychohistory. There were more routes to the past than ever before. Yet the study of history remained a private enterprise, the historian's choice, always an expression of today's needs rather than the pure voice of the past.

So, for example, it was surely no accident that the early practitioners of the new social history shared certain private preoccupations: They were, like me, new parents and keenly interested in childhood and the problems of socialization; nearly all of them, like me, were experiencing degrees of marital strife. At the same time, the spirit of dissent was encouraging the rise of a radical history. As New Left graduates joined the academic professions, the vocabulary of Marx and Marcuse entered the historical jargon.

A radical history "caucus" offered relevant bibliographies and seminars, and eventually launched its distinctive publications. On yet another front was the rapid expansion of women's history, particularly the proliferation of women's studies programs that outflanked the old guard of the historical profession. (My own department employed no tenure-track women.) Of course, women's history was not necessarily radical; to focus on pots and pans, the trivia of the dispossessed, too easily distracted attention from power relationships. But given the overwhelming domination of American history (and the historical profession) by male Anglo-Protestants, the very appearance of outgroups (women, minorities, workers) constituted a subversive trend.

Instinctively, I turned to the new history in search of reconciliation, though at the time it seemed to be only a delightful, extraordinary coincidence: the personal frustrations of a fledgling historian converging with my discovery of what surely was the first serious student rebellion in American history. But, of course, nothing is purely coincidental. What we historians "discover"—what captures our imagination in the sources—always reflects our contemporary concerns. The student uprising I found in the archives had nothing to do with black studies or the draft; it focused, rather, on science and "natural philosophy." But in this obscure campus rebellion, not very different from the student protests of the 1960s, I saw an opportunity to resolve the contradictions of my education as a historian. I also found a way to spend more time inside my three private offices, conveniently evading the facts of life outside.

To understand the unfolding irony we must travel two and a half centuries and more: The time is 1717, the setting Yale College, then an infant "school of the prophets," which had recently moved its classes from the seacoast town of Saybrook to a new location at New Haven. Yale had been founded in 1701 by the local ministers to serve as a bulwark of Puritan orthodoxy against the invasion of secular ideas associated with the Age of Reason. Students pursued a traditional liberal arts education (the classics, philosophy, the disputory arts) as well as the theological verities necessary to enter an ecclesiastical profession, though, of course, not every graduate would choose that line of work. The curriculum, in any case, mirrored the prevailing wisdom of the Puritan clergy. An observer of the Yale commencement of 1714 remarked "that all knotty questions (although twisted as hard as the Gordian one) may be resolved and untied; and that they'll do it, although with Alexander's sword." And "for their reward," he added, "they shall have . . . an empire, but not of the known world, but of the unknown world."

While the Yale graduates were glorifying their intelligence, however, certain unexpected and unplanned acts of subversion were about to destroy the foundations of the Puritan intellectual heritage. In 1714 Connecticut's agent in London, Jeremiah Dummer, procured a sizable library of new books for the college. These volumes included what was known as "the new learning"—the works of Newton, Locke, Boyle, and other modern thinkers. Their arrival in Connecticut quickly disrupted the complacency of provincial intellectuals. One Yale tutor, Samuel Johnson (class of 1714)—a distant relation of the famous English lexicographer of the same name—described the Dummer library as "a flood of day to his low state of mind."

Samuel Johnson and some of the students and teachers promptly immersed themselves in the Dummer collection, striving to incorporate the new learning into their way of looking at the world. But when they actually changed the undergraduate curriculum to accommodate the new philosophy in 1717, the students erupted in protest. (Among the rebels was the young Jonathan Edwards, destined to become the foremost evangelical minister and philosopher in colonial America.) Mistrustful of Johnson's reforms, the undergraduates refused to attend classes. It required a formal act of the colony government to end the resistance, and one of the casualties of the fiasco was Samuel Johnson, who tendered his resignation.

Johnson's defeat, when added to the original discovery of the new learning, greatly weakened his confidence in Puritan values. He now began to question the validity of the Puritan religious system itself—the "New England way" established by John Winthrop's generation nearly a century earlier. His doubts culminated at the Yale commencement in 1722, when he and seven coconspirators boldly announced their conversion to the episcopal Church of England, the very church the Puritan founders had fled into the wilderness to escape. "The heavens opened and consternation rained down," wrote Perry Miller of the episode. "They had read the books in Dummer's gift; they had compared these weighty arguments and noble styles with provincial sparseness, had mediated upon the disorders and confusion of Congregationalism, and perceived the strength, dignity, and majesty of apostolic succession."

The Yale Apostasy, as the dramatic announcement was known, thus symbolized a fundamental transformation of American culture: once the "city uppon a hill," the vanguard of human history, colonial New England, in just three generations, had become a sleepy province cut off from the glory and sophistication of the metropolitan mainstream. No wonder Samuel Johnson and his ilk preferred the Church of England. For historians like Miller, then, the conversions served as a curious episode in the larger process of cultural change.

Reading about the Yale Apostasy in the 1960s, that other era of student dissent and political crisis, I found myself asking questions about the protagonists: Why had the young Samuel Johnson (and a tiny handful of friends) been so willing to repudiate the dominant values of his culture? What had caused so profound an alienation? How had he attained the strength of character to challenge and defy the entire structure of authority? And how had he felt about his actions and the ensuing crisis? How did it *feel to be hated* by most of one's peers and neighbors? What, I wondered, was the emotional underpinning of this dramatic decision? These were the Insoluble Problems that initially intrigued me.

Much later, I would realize that my fascination with the Yale Apostasy reflected the parallel crisis of my own career. But what led me first to Samuel Johnson was the abundance of documentary evidence he had left behind. In the course of his long life (1696–1772), Johnson enjoyed a certain renown. Besides his early success at Yale and his notorious conversion, he was a tireless missionary for the Church of England, preaching regularly throughout the colony; he published numerous tracts, sermons, and essays as well as the first philosophy textbook in American history (used at Benjamin Franklin's college in Philadelphia); and he served as the first president of King's College in New York City (the forerunner of Columbia University). His personal papers comprised sermons, diaries, letters, unpublished essays, and a detailed autobiography. Herein rested a solid archive with which to address the questions of motivation ignored by previous historians.

Here too was a way to reconcile my own academic training with the new social history of the late 1960s. From Johnson's voluminous writings it was fairly easy to reconstruct his state of mind: what he believed, what he valued, how he looked at the world, and not least, what he thought of himself. Such information fell into the category of "intellectual" history, with which I was familiar. Meanwhile, the work of the social historians had sketched out the patterns of colonial family life: how households functioned, how children were nurtured and socialized, how child-rearing related to behavioral norms. Because Johnson had preserved considerable evidence about his own family life and had written extensively about child-rearing and pedagogy, it seemed possible to compare his personal experience with the larger historical trends.

What appeared as a convenient bridge between the two territories—the intellectual and the social—was another burgeoning field known as "psychohistory." The term originated in the science-fiction writing of Isaac Asimov—and that, I thought, should be a sufficient caveat against its hasty acceptance. (More than one colleague delighted in asking if it were true I'd become a "psycho" historian.) Psychohistory nevertheless offered the possibility of exploring the relationship between an individual life and the broad swings of history. It also promised an understanding of what might be called the emotional past—the feelings, mood, and ambience of an age—which, after all, must have constituted a basic ingredient of the cultural reality.

Historians, I soon found, distrust psychohistory. It frightens them, largely because it introduces the question of the unconscious. They do not like to deal with facts that are hard to prove, and what is unconscious, by definition, is not readily available to cross-checking and contemporary comment. The working assumption for most historians, rather, is that the people they study should respond emotionally to events in the same way they would themselves, a commonsense psychology based on the historian's own sense of what is "normal." The idea that the human mind may be irrational—no one would totally dismiss it—just adds too much uncertainty to the historical picture.

For Samuel Johnson and colonial New England, the logic of psychohistory seemed straightforward. If we accepted the fact that he was a child of his times—bred and raised inside a particular family and influenced by its values—then it was reasonable to assume that there might be some relationship between his upbringing and his subsequent choices as an adult: what he came to do with his life, what he believed, how he related to his society. In other words, we might expect a convergence between his personality and his mature acts and beliefs. Child-rearing did not necessarily cause Johnson to become who he was, but certainly it would have narrowed his choices and established boundaries about acceptable conduct. Yet Samuel Johnson had *not* become a well-socialized individual; his apostasy represented a total rejection of his upbringing. Why had that happened?

Johnson's genealogy, I found, closely mirrored the cultural events described by historians like Perry Miller. His grandfather was named William Johnson and had been one of the Puritan Fathers, much respected and adored by his friends, neighbors, and descendants, including his eldest grandchild, Samuel Johnson. But William Johnson's son (Samuel Johnson's father), also named Samuel Johnson, lacked the eminence of the old man. At least that is the way the younger Samuel Johnson viewed his family history. From his grandfather, moreover, Samuel Johnson acquired (as he wrote in his autobiography) "an impatient curiosity to know everything that could be known." This "thirst after knowledge and truth" became "his ruling passion" and led him through the doors of Yale at the age of fourteen in 1710. Young Johnson's success at the college enabled him to indulge his adolescent fantasies of becoming the most knowledgeable man in the world. (I found marginal annotations in one of his notebooks, in which the vain undergraduate described himself, in Latin no less, as "Samuel the wise, the virtuous, Johnson.")

The abrupt arrival of the Dummer library from England thus represented not just an intellectual surprise but an emotional blow as well. For the existence of "new learning" showed unmistakably that no matter how erudite Johnson might appear in New England, in reality he was a small fish in the British pond. His initial response—much like my own grasping at psychohistory—was to attempt to incorporate the new learning into the old Yale curriculum. But this step provoked the student rebellion and cost him his job. So if Samuel Johnson hoped to fulfill his childhood ambitions to become the most learned man in the world (a fantasy, be it noted, that he had derived from his Puritan grandfather), it became necessary for him to overcome the limits of the provincial identity. In other words, to satisfy his basic psychological impulses (the identification with his grandfather and the dream of the city on a hill), he had to reject the very establishment that had inspired his ambition; he would look for better models in the Church of England.

This explanation of the Yale Apostasy did not contradict the traditional version. But it did add an entire substrate of meaning —an emotional, even unconscious level of motivation. It revealed the hidden logic of Johnson's development: why he risked his entire career, why he suffered so long the hatred of his neighbors, why in the ensuing five decades his creative career took the direction it did. Nor had I stepped outside history to elaborate the evidence. Although my analysis of Johnson's life depended upon modern psychological themes—such concepts as narcissism, the reversal of generations, Erikson's identity crisis—the conclusions did not require ahistorical leaps of faith. Johnson's personality development, as I portrayed it, remained rooted in the institutions and intellectual framework of Puritan New England.

To present psychohistory in such reasoned academic garb, however, belies its most subversive tendency. When a student asked why I had chosen to write about Samuel Johnson, I rendered the

usual scholarly reply: the significance of the issues, the avail-
ability of sources, the Insoluble Problem. But when the student
asked, more earnestly, why I had *really* chosen Samuel Johnson,
I realized there had to be a deeper relationship between the crisis
of 1722 and my twentieth-century circumstances.

Freudians talk about the frequency of "overdetermination": the
simultaneity of multiple causes. All my stated reasons for writing
about Samuel Johnson were true, but to my surprise I discovered
that there were others I hadn't consciously considered. I remembered, for example, that a conversion experience in Connecticut
had occurred once in my own family, causing, in part, the unhappy relationship between my father and his brother. This uncle
was the history buff in the family, my father once said, as he remarked about my physical resemblance to his brother. Like my
uncle, moreover, I had fallen in love with a woman from Connecticut, whose name, amazingly, was almost the same! All these
"coincidences" moved in a single direction. Had I identified—un-
consciously, to be sure—with my uncle as a way of establishing
some independence from my parents? My father's absolute re-
fusal to discuss such a possibility certainly made it seem plausible
(to me). Even more compelling was the similarity of my ignorance of "the new learning" of the 1960s: In no small measure,
Johnson and I had wound up in the same academic cul-de-sac.
Was my interest in Samuel Johnson a projection of my personal
crisis? Were my conclusions the extension of the same problems?
And having conceded these points, what did they mean?

Historians, like other scholars, strive to be objective, even as
they deny the possibility of being so. They admit that each generation will write its own history (because each generation asks its
own questions of the past), and then they go about their activities
as though what they are writing will last for all time. Psychohistory, by contrast, questions the pretense. Instead of saying
that one's subjective feelings are deceptive and therefore best left
repressed, a psychohistorian attempts to bring the unconscious
into consciousness, where its usefulness and validity might be
weighed along with other, more familiar types of inspiration. My
interpretation of Samuel Johnson's special relationship with his

grandfather, for example, showed a curious parallel to the feelings I had for my own grandpa. Perhaps that's what enabled me to empathize with him so well. Such subjectivity, I thought, should be seen not as an obstacle but as a source of insight. Without my personal experience I probably never would have considered that aspect of Johnson's biography. In any event, there is no advantage in pretending that my mind did not exist.

Psychohistory, in this light, emerged in the late 1960s as an academic counterpart to the antiestablishment counterculture. Like the hippie movement of the time, psychohistory was questioning the emphasis upon objectivity, rationality, and specialization. Here, I believed, was its tremendous potential. For one thing, psychohistory cut across the traditional disciplines, merging history, psychology, sociology, anthropology, and literary criticism. In my psychohistory seminar I could teach all those subjects at the same time. Psychohistory also denied the separation of the inquiring mind from the facts "out there." It focused on history's irrationality—feelings, emotions, passions—topics that seldom enter scholarly conversation. And by stressing the reciprocal relationship between scholar and subject, psychohistory suggested that the proper unit of study was both: To do history well, we all had to acknowledge our historicity, our own entrapment in the here and now.

True, I'd spent a couple of years following Samuel Johnson through the archives. I could document and footnote every statement I made about him. Indeed, I could never have understood the man so well had I attempted to short circuit the arduous process of research. But in the end, my best insights were intuitive, the result of my own irrational, unconscious development. All the academic trappings notwithstanding, my depiction of Samuel Johnson might well have been a self-portrait and my historical analysis an oblique autobiography. I never intended that result. And yet, isn't that what all history should mean? Don't we pursue the past the better to understand ourselves?

As I considered the paradox, I was forced to make one more concession. My biography of Johnson did not stop at the moment of his conversion; I had also traced his career until his death fifty years later—a time of loneliness, rejection, frustration. If his story was in any way a model for my own, I had to confront such possibilities. To turn my back on colleagues and career as Johnson did promised little reward and much difficulty. I too would abandon security, lose the favors of institutional support, and discover the uncertainty and fear of working alone. It was a sobering prospect. While pursuing the Johnson project, I had put aside such choices, buried myself in the past, bought time. So when, at last, I was done with Samuel Johnson, I was surprised to realize that I'd already made up my mind, effortlessly. I would follow my subject, declare independence.

ELEVEN

The Professional Style

I fashioned the perfect escape from Clio's clutches. Just before bidding adieu to academia, I absconded with the funds— except in the university they call such loot a fellowship. No longer was I seeking the perfect footnote, but rather an explanation of how and why I had become embedded in the academic world in the first place. I called my new project "Graduate Education in the Historical Profession," because that is how one gets grants. But what I actually was doing was finding and interviewing my former classmates from graduate school to discover what had happened to their lives. It would be a white-collar version of Roger Kahn's book about the aging Brooklyn Dodgers, *Boys of Summer;* we were the Boys of Autumn.

In September 1964 my classmates and I—about twenty of us in all—began our professional training with lofty visions of the academic potential. We were assured by our mentors that we could obtain Ph.D. degrees in history, providing we followed the prescribed, though demanding, program of study. We were assured by the larger society that people with advanced degrees would always be necessary to the national welfare and that we would never have to worry about employment and security. And we assured ourselves that our professional expertise would make a significant contribution to American life.

My own fortunes epitomized the best and the worst of those

promises. Despite my many frustrations with the historical profession, I enjoyed more freedom than anyone else I knew. I could
teach what and when I wanted. In my last year at Minnesota I
fulfilled *all* my responsibilities by offering two seminars that met
every Wednesday for two hours. The remainder of the time was
my own, accountable to no one. Nothing short of "moral turpi-
tude" could jeopardize my independence. Here, surely, was one
measure of success.

My future was so secure, however, that I had no future at
all. In forty-three years, in the year 2012 to be exact, I would
reach mandatory retirement age, which, with my family's medical
history, exceeded the actuarial expectation. My career extended
to the horizons of time, forever unchanging, forever the same.
So instead of feeling free, I experienced entrapment. I felt obligated, first, to my institution—colleagues, committees, students
—which, of course, was the raison d'etre of academic tenure.
Having given all, it could claim all.

I sought alternatives off campus, but that only accentuated the
incongruities of my professional identity, the image of the scholar.
The role defined who I was to the world outside. It never seemed
like me. I was always embarrassed by the luxuries of the lifestyle
and the dubious value of the work. I always felt like someone
living unfairly on welfare. I wanted instead a vocation that was
more worldly, more "real," something that seemed—to use the
parlance of the times—more relevant.

What had gone wrong? I pondered the choices that led me to
this moment of resolution. Why had I been so enthralled with
the world of scholarship? And why now was I not? Was my predicament personal, which is to say psychological? Or was I, like
all historical subjects, a product of the times? My instincts told
me to look to the past, seek answers in origins, explore the true
beginnings. So I began to contact the people who knew me best
in that earlier time.

As I crossed the continent—Toronto to Georgia, North Carolina to Los Angeles—I was struck first by how much had *not*
changed in the intervening ten years. Usually I was greeted
warmly, treated as a breath of air from the past, and permitted

to reestablish familiar bonds of friendship. We were veterans of the same academic rituals: Insoluble Problems and boozy parties, seminars, examinations, and dissertations. So my former class-mates gave generously of their views and their intimacies, en-joying the opportunity to rehash old grievances, share moments of triumph, or confess various sins of the heart and body. By carefully cross-checking their accounts, moreover, I could cor-roborate their claims and even acquire additional details or alter-nate versions of the same events. Some of them contributed old correspondence, diaries, and miscellaneous memorabilia to my burgeoning archive. But because the true focus of my study was myself—my career mirrored in theirs—I could never bring myself to publish the results.

Finding my classmates ten years later, in the early 1970s, I discovered at once that my dissatisfactions with academia were hardly original. Most of my friends, then in their early thirties, divided about equally between those who were successful profes-sionals—writing books and articles, directing dissertations, win-ning fellowships—and those who for reasons of personality or opportunity had switched careers. Some had washed out of the Ph.D. program—despite all the optimistic promises—and some had been unwilling or unable to make the personal adjustments required by graduate study. A few, like me, just quit their jobs to find more satisfying careers. But what soon became apparent from my interviews was that these choices were less the result of rational decision-making—the desire for money, security, pres-tige, or convenience—than they were a search for psychological equilibrium.

I heard two anecdotes that best illuminate the issue: the dog and cat stories.

The first involves a dark-haired, chubby, Jewish man from a midwestern suburb, who was married to a schoolteacher. Be-cause she was working on what was sarcastically called the Ph.T.—Putting Hubby Through—they had a bit more discretionary in-come than most of us. One day, he decided to splurge; he bought his wife a German shepherd puppy. Like many childless couples, they were soon treating Fido as next of kin. But one morning, a school day as it turned out, Fido fell ill: vomiting, shivering, showing other symptoms of distemper, which is usually a fatal disease. The wife was at work; my friend was already frantic about a seminar report that was due in the afternoon. What to do? He pretended the dog was not sick. Then he grew angry and put the whimpering dog in a closet, but the whines were ruining his concentration. At last, he cradled the dog in his arms and took him by bus to the vet. There was no cure, and the dog, as they say, was put to sleep. But my friend had failed to finish his report. In the seminar, he told me, he was "ripped to shreds." With a poor grade he could not renew his fellowship. He left graduate school. When I found him ten years later, he was working as an insurance adjuster in Baltimore. His retrospective view of graduate school compared with the reminiscences of an ex-con.

As for the cat, one day she made the mistake of walking across a desktop littered with the paraphernalia of research. Her owner, a bright, blond man with a promising academic career, was preparing frantically for his oral examinations. Infuriated by the interruption, he grabbed the cat by the tail and threw her against the wall. She died instantly. When I last heard of him, he had just obtained a tenured job.

These are true stories—graphic almost to sentimentality. But that is because it's sometimes easier to empathize with a dog and a cat. Imagine how these people treated their families. And my interviews unlocked similar types of stories that permitted me to reach certain generalizations about life inside academia, and after.

The professors I visited were generally more comfortable and unabashedly more smug than the nonacademics. Slightly ahead of the baby boomers and the demand for teachers, they rode like surfers across the crest of the expanding academic marketplace. Most were then on the verge of tenure—that mystical state of everlasting security, equivalent to Winthrop's "sainthood"— and since my interviews, all have achieved it. Never again need they worry about material concerns; although, of course, being human, they do. One of them told the story of a California professor who, in the days when Ronald Reagan was governor of the state, was asked how much work he had to do to justify the luxury of tenure.

"Nine hours," replied the educator.

"Well, it's a long day," commented the investigator, "but the work is easy." No one bothered to inform him that "nine hours" referred not to the workday but the workweek! (And, yes, most serious academics spend far more time on their professional duties than that, though they never have to justify exactly what they do.)

The common denominator among the academic professionals was not too hard to find. Other people, when they are drinking, talk about politics or sports or sex. But as the academics became mellow they talked mostly about their research. Some had embarked on the new history and took considerable pride in their ability to grow with the territory; some were still trying to solve the old Insoluble Problems. Either way, they held an abiding commitment to their work, the self-confident assurance that the study of History required no special justifications. It was good in itself. And a few of them admitted, half-apologetically to be sure, a taste for administration.

But this love of scholarship, I observed, also revealed a surprising sexual dimension. Screwed and screwing appeared as a constant theme, though seldom in the erotic sense. About one-third of my classmates had neither married nor established enduring sexual relationships of any sort. Three of them—men in their mid-thirties—admitted to being virgins! Three were living in homosexual closets; at least one of them has since come out. Of those who had married, nearly one-half also had been divorced. By way of explanation, one of my classmates remarked with a nervous laugh that the professors probably expended their best bodily fluids in the archives. A commitment to scholarship, he added, not only encouraged all kinds of antisocial impulses; it excused them, even necessitated them. There was always one more footnote.

My nonacademic classmates, meanwhile, claimed to feel relief to be out of the university pressure cooker. When I visited their homes, they were still new to their careers and so less affluent than the professors, but their prospects were much brighter. Most had white-collar jobs in the private sector. In some ways they led simpler lives: They were homebodies. They watched more TV, ate at fewer restaurants, read books for pleasure. When they smoked, they preferred tobacco to pot, and they consumed more beer than whiskey.

The nonacademics, however, lacked one major luxury. They did not have tax-deductible offices in their homes—retreats that lured and sheltered them from contact with their families and friends. When they abandoned the quest for the holy footnote, alas, they surrendered the excuse of "research." Ironically, too, the nonacademics clung to an idealized image of the university "community," as if a spirit of collegiality really did reign on American campuses. Such illusions showed how remote they really were from their former lives. After all, when you get right down to it, the major fights in the university do not address great theoretical issues; they involve the basics: hiring, firing, tenure, promotion, and salaries!

In Skokie, Illinois, there was a rather tense housewife in her mid-thirties named Marsha, still suffering from her failure in graduate school. (She begged me to use her full name "so they would know how they ruined my life.") She had gained weight since I last saw her; her skin was splotchy. It was obvious that she was victimized by much more than an academic decision that prevented her from completing a Ph.D. Her husband never respected her—which was why, she said, she'd enrolled in graduate school in the first place; her children made fun of her stammer. A few weeks before I arrived, her psychiatrist died, leaving her miserably alone. I remembered Sarah as a slightly befuddled student, frantically juggling course work and housework. She was a convenient target for our male mirth. What did we know about family responsibilities? Now, with tears running down her cheeks, she rummaged through some cartons in the basement for copies of her correspondence with the chairman of the department, a man I remembered as a courtly old gentleman. "Academic dismissal," she sobbed. "Why wouldn't they listen to me?"

How could they listen? Few in the academic world cared to address such personal problems. The professional style preferred other values: detachment and objectivity, the separation of feelings from judgment. Seldom was the division successful, of course, and scholars have allowed deep passions to slip into their work. Among my professorial friends, for example, I detected the same kinds of emotional influences, some of them scarcely conscious, that had surfaced in my study of the young Samuel Johnson: The Jews became experts in Christian history; ex-athletes studied military heroes; the fatherless wrote about strong authority figures. They seemed perplexed, then amused, when I suggested these connections; none really protested. But despite any private confessions, within academia such expressions of the self are considered flaws, human errors best kept under control, especially around students. (Ironically, as one professor reminded me, graduate students love to imitate the professional style. My wife called it ass-kissing. But we believed in, desired, that mystique of formal detachment.)

Near Boulder, Colorado, I interviewed Steve, a former history teacher and now a dishwasher in a ski resort, where he had fled after some state troopers opened fire on a peace march he had organized, killing one of his students. The snow-covered mountains and thick pines surrounded his rented cabin with a sublime tranquility, but he could find no peace there. He angrily denied the suggestion that he was running away from the political realities at sea level. "I knew the risks I was taking when I gave a speech," he said. "But I can't be responsible for what happens when my students come out to listen." He had destroyed his half-finished dissertation—as well as the notes necessary to reconstruct it. His decision to leave academia, unlike mine, was irreversible. Yet he believed he still had much to teach, which made his anger profound and unquenchable. Only much later did he trust himself to come down from the mountain. When last I heard of him, around 1980, he was apprenticing to become a stock-market analyst.

I met Jack in London, where he was finishing research for a book about rural reform and the Enclosure Movement in England. He invited me to his flat in Earl's Court Road for dinner, and we consumed abundant scotch while we waited for his wife to come home. She had been an undergraduate when they married in the mid-1960s—tall, slender, clear-skinned as a model. "Drat," she said as the door bumped open. She apologized for the delay, then disappeared into the small kitchen while Jack droned on about his research, explaining how the enclosure of sheep within fences increased the uses of sheep shit. Eventually, the chicken arrived undercooked, but we were in no condition to care. Then, somewhere in the monologue about the uses of sheep shit, Jack's wife went to bed.

A phone call the next morning wrenched me from a stupor: Jack's wife was asking to come over. She turned out to be an authority on the "enclosure movement," as it were, and had decided to return to the open fields. She asked me to break the news to Jack, which I declined, and then to help carry her luggage to another flat, which seemed more reasonable. When the move was completed, Jack expressed great relief. He promptly put aside his research, lost about thirty pounds, and spent the remainder of the summer chasing women. For my benefit he wrote a long memoir about his sexual escapades—he was not exactly one of those virgins—and presented it to me the night before he left for America. By the time I visited him in his hometown the next year, he had married a young widow. We drank scotch while we waited for her to make dinner, and somewhere in the monologue about the uses of sheep shit she went to bed.

The second wives were not always identical to the prototypes. Even so, one former classmate would never call his new wife by name lest he blunder and summon up the wrong one. Although these new wives were usually a little younger, they seemed less ornamental and strove to maintain their independent interests. Perhaps, then, they required less attention than did their predecessors, for these second marriages have mostly endured.

The ex-wives, when I found them later, remained bitter, even when they had initiated the divorces. Most had remarried, but not to academics. For them, the sacrifices of graduate school, followed by the claustrophobia of faculty wife status, had added up to nil. In all cases they took their children with them, leaving the men, like me, far away to play daddy in the summers. By contrast, there was not a single divorce among the nonacademic couples.

The last stop, as I planned it, was in the Pacific Northwest, where Bill, a high-school jock-turned-historian had relocated at a small liberal arts college after his divorce. (Ten years earlier, it was Bill who saved my neck when I claimed, prematurely, to have solved Uncle Frank's Insoluble WHERE WAS THE BATTLE OF SARATOGA FOUGHT?) A native of the Midwest, he was thriving far from home—and far from his first wife—although he claimed merely to have grown up with the times. The Beatles and Rolling Stones poured from his high-tech stereo; he was developing a multimedia show to use in a new course on the history of rock'n'roll. While I was there, his house was besieged by students, who brought term papers, borrowed books, or just dropped by to say hello and share a joint. For all the casualness, however, Bill held firmly to the old academic standards. He was known as a tough grader, for which his students seemed to respect him. "I'm totally into teaching," he explained. "I'll probably never write one damn scholarly article."

The day before I left, Bill and I shared a mild tab of LSD and together set off across some dry, barren land near his house. It was a golden, sunny April day; the first smell of spring was in the air. We threw sticks and pebbles at imaginary targets and marveled at the beauty of a hawk in flight. He spoke wistfully about the years in graduate school, the ease of being completely dependent on decisions we could not control: grades, letters of recommendation, the job market.

"Right now," I asked, "do you feel that you could close your eyes and be back there again? Exactly as it was?"

Bill glared at me—moved as if to throw a rock at my skull. "Never. It was the worst time of my life."

Who can say where or when it began?

The academic womb that kept us dependent gave us plenty of security. There are not many places that offer lifetime tenure before you're thirty, and not many places that expect you to work a six- or eight-hour week, and not many places that pay you to do whatever you want (in the name of academic freedom) and encourage you to take time off to do it better. What justified such luxuries was a medieval tradition—the privileges of a clergy that could read and write—which in the modern world translated into a belief that scholarly activities, however peculiar or arcane, were inherently more valuable than other worldly pursuits, including one's private life. Yet, ironically, the academic society that embraced my classmates appeared little different from other bureaucratic institutions that take over one's life.

In a recent alumni report I noticed that the intellectual productivity among my classmates has declined. They are writing fewer books and articles, presenting fewer papers, doing less history. Some have again switched fields. More have become department chairmen and deans. Whatever their idealism and sincerity, they now seem less committed to their subject than to the institutions that support them. Their lives are secure. They are unlikely to make great leaps. As for the nonacademics, I find they do not usually reply to the annual alumni questionnaire.

The report served to validate my own choice. The decision to leave the comforts of the academic tower reflected a desire to be less privileged, to live a little closer to the mundanities of the times. I no longer wanted to feel embarrassed about the short workweek, the largesse of the public dole (those marvelous, tax-free grants), or the relevance of my research. I would try, instead, to take my sense of history outside the university, where I might translate the subject into a vernacular voice. For my quarrel was never with History—the flow of time that enmeshes all human life—but only with a profession that had claimed it as its own.

PART THREE

Moving Out

California

TWELVE

Living in Sin

I arrived in California by way of Spain; it was one of those in-
auspicious detours that forever change your life. It began as a
vacation the first summer after my separation, a fling, really.
Alice was going to the coast of southern Spain to ferret out her
family roots and suggested I meet her there. We were not exactly
strangers. She also had been married for the proverbial seven
years. She also wanted no entangling alliances. And in Spain,
disconnected from our recent history, we might explore our own
terra incognita, seemingly without the usual risks.

But if Spain evoked for Alice happy memories of her grandparents, Gustavo and Leonides, a young couple who sailed on the
Aida from Gibraltar to Brooklyn in 1911, for me Spain aroused
a more ominous mood. Franco was still alive; the Guardia Civil
paraded everywhere in pairs, carrying machine guns. I'd been
warned not to visit this vestige of 1930s fascism; my father, once
a supporter of the anti-Franco Friends of the Abraham Lincoln
Battalion, refused to contribute one tourist peseta to the dictator's
economy. I was passionately curious about the civil war, however,
and passionate, too, about Alice.

With such mixed motives, my historical investigations
remained quite limited. I was struck, in fact, by how little tangible evidence of the civil war I could actually observe—except
the fear. And, of course, no one would speak openly to a stranger,

even if I had dared to ask questions, which I did not. Just a few years later, after Franco was dead, I returned to Spain and saw not only the unrepaired shambles of the war in such places as Guernica, but also interviewed numerous "ex-presos," victims of the Franco regime, some of whom had spent twenty years and more in his barbaric prisons. Was I too cautious on my first trip? Or merely preoccupied?

Despite our best intentions to avoid long-term risks, Alice and I seemed to get along very well indeed. In Spain, where we were unbound by familiar conventions—old friends, former spouses, our pasts—we discovered a shared nonchalance about middle-class proprieties. One afternoon we crashed the posh Hotel Alfonso X in Seville, blithely expropriating stationery and instructing a curious waiter to bring us gin and tonics. We enjoyed passing as guests. It proved we could still resume our middle-class habits if ever we chose to do so. We might still go home again—both geographically and spiritually. But could we resist the temptation? Could we sustain that healthy irreverence after we returned to our normal environment, when we had to confront, once again, our separate histories?

On our last Sunday in Barcelona we sat on our hotel balcony overlooking the fabled Ramblas, a broad boulevard filled with trees, flowers, and singing birds, and contemplated our options. We did not want history to repeat itself; we did not want to become another unhappily married couple. "Marriage," declared Alice with a marvelous scorn, "is based on the illusion that you can institutionalize the future."

We knew that from experience. As products of the 1950s, we had assumed (in the sense that one assumes a new position) that marriage was a stage of human development, part of the inevitable process of moving from childhood through puberty to adulthood. It was natural. We grew up and got married, all in the same breath. Except that during the 1960s certain unexpected social trends had converged to illuminate a crucial distinction between what was "natural" and what was "historical." The roots were clearly delineated in the old *Kinsey Report:* A remarkable number of otherwise respectable American men and women were sexually frustrated and willing to cheat, even commit crimes, to achieve sexual satisfaction. At the same time, the traditional family structure was undermined by the rise of a service economy that redefined "male" jobs and encouraged ever-larger numbers of women to enter the work force. A simultaneous crisis of cultural values—the specter of the bomb, the demand for equal rights, the generation gap—underscored the arbitrary nature of existing expectations. Couldn't we start a new history?

We decided to experiment. Amid the clamor about the death of the American family in the 1960s and early 1970s, certain countertrends were emerging. For one thing, divorced people seem to remarry with remarkable ease—80 percent for men, 75 percent for women, within two years. Under the doctrine of "no-fault" divorce, moreover, second marriages often served as convenient stepping-stones to marriage number three, and so on. Thus in the 1970s the notion of "serial monogamy" was perfected. Alice and I had no interest in participating in that movement. Having been to the altar once, having pledged unto eternity, and having broken those vows, it was hard to imagine any later promises proving more binding. Besides, all the familiar reasons that justified a conventional living arrangement—the law, morality, social convenience—seemed to be artificial obstacles to the simple desire to create a voluntaristic relationship.

So we did nothing. Which, as it turns out, also formed part of a historical trend in this country. There is no precise terminology to describe it, but the Census Bureau abbreviates the phenomenon POSSLQ (People of the Opposite Sex Sharing Living Quarters). And their statistics suggest that our numbers have more than quadrupled since 1970. By the mid-1980s we comprised over 2 million households, some 2 percent of the national total. But even these figures probably underestimate the trend, ignoring people who maintain at least some semblance of a separate domicile as well as the rising number of gay households, which, by definition, don't count. This alternative apparently appeals primarily to people at the extremes of the age spectrum: young adults just beginning their sexual relationships and the elderly, who seem particularly fearful of surrendering their independence to a marital arrangement. Neither category quite fit Alice and me.

Living in sin: I am drawn to that lusty metaphor, the image of sexual outlaws clutched together in a dusky hotel room near the Mediterranean, impervious to the bullhorn calls for surrender from the moral posse outside. No longer does that film noir image explain why, after all this time, I still live with the woman I met up with in Málaga in that summer of 1972. But no other explanation can ignore that primordial pull to live on the frontiers of propriety.

Alice and I did not start out being fanatic about not getting married. At first we were just gun-shy, afraid of plunging into another relationship. We played for time. By not finalizing our legal divorces, we also resolved many of the questions of our outlaw status: the need to keep separate accounts, insurance policies, our names. But very soon a variety of minor hassles—signing rental agreements, straightening out the mailman, the decline of social invitations—stiffened our attitude. Our vaguely defined mistrust of marriage deepened into a coherent defense of our marital alternative.

We became, frankly, obsessed with preserving all aspects of free choice. We chose our own friends; we would allow neither to commit the other to a social engagement. Because we wanted to live by desire rather than by rules, we refused even to create rules of self-government. In the first issue of *Ms.* magazine, published late in 1971, just a few months before our rendezvous in Spain, the novelist Alix Kates Shulman presented for public scrutiny a copy of her "liberated" marriage contract—a compendium of mutual privileges and responsibilities that purported to eliminate the exploitative aspect of housework. (Actually, it was a postmarriage contract, proving our suspicion that in a bureaucratic mind one set of rules leads logically to another.)

We wouldn't consider it. Contractual relations, even with the best of attorneys, assume a formal structure that contradicted our romantic sense of trust. In a free relationship, we decided, our duties did not have to be spelled out like a fourth-grade lesson plan, a tradeoff of chores—washing for drying, dusting for vacuuming, the sink for the toilet. Instead, we both agreed to be responsible, to do what we could, and to trust our love to provide a natural equalization. Fortunately, too, as my mother liked to say, neither of us worked for the Board of Health.

We also tried to cultivate friendships with other unmarried couples—hoping that a common unmarital status would provide the basis for an alternative kinship. There was no shortage of such people, at first. But for reasons that always baffled us, most of these friends eventually decided to tie the knot. According to the census statistics, that also seems to be a growing trend; an estimated one-third of all POSSLQ relationships culminate in failure, which is to say marriage. Perhaps in the not-so-distant future cohabitation will serve as an amoral equivalent to engagement—an untimid posting of the banns—in which couples realistically appraise their compatibility. Among our friends, these belated marriages sometimes lasted long enough for them to reach the next plateau: divorce. Then the cycle might start again.

Here was another subject of historical debate. The liberalization of divorce laws did not extend to unmarried couples. My status had no legal protection; I couldn't divorce Alice if I wanted to, or lay claim to any hidden treasure. Although certain agencies of the federal government, such as the Department of Housing and Urban Development, granted equal status to unmarried couples (if they maintained a "stable family relationship"), the states were usually more conservative, in many places treating cohabitation as a crime. In such matters, however, California set the pace. In a precedent-breaking decision (the Lee Marvin "palimony" case of 1977), the California Supreme Court ruled that couples who engaged in sexual relationships outside marriage did not forfeit their standing before the law. Thus living-together contracts, written or oral, prevailed over traditional moral considerations. Alice and I could be saved, after all, by the sanctity of contracts, if we had one.

The invention of new family styles in the seventies also stimulated a growing enthusiasm for enlarging the two-person household. After twenty years' decline, the national birthrate stabilized

in 1975 and then began to creep upward. By the end of the decade
the country was experiencing a veritable baby boom, particularly
among older couples who had delayed first marriages or sought
to solidify later relationships. Thanks to medical technology, the
possibility of averting birth defects made these decisions much
easier than in the past.

To my astonishment, Alice began to succumb to a peculiar craving, what Phyllis Schlafly calls "baby hunger." She wanted a child.
The issue was far less pressing to me. Having abandoned custody
of one son, I was understandably not anxious to risk another. I
also doubted whether our anti-institutional lifestyle could withstand the structure a child would require. I had been through it
before. But here we were, nearing forty and the mid-life crisis,
feeling that time was running out. It was our pride that drove us
to it. We wanted to perpetuate, if we could, the special chemistry
that held us together.

We grappled first with the legal implications of having a child
out of wedlock. We knew we could resolve these matters easily
enough: We could always get married. But the legal issues—legitimacy, paternity, inheritance—seemed so irrelevant to our desire to have a baby. Moreover, our outlaw status had become, over
the years, an integral part of our identity. It helped us define who
we were, to ourselves, to each other, to everyone else. Marriage
was quite incompatible with that self-image.

Nor, as we both knew from experience, could a legal marriage provide any greater security against a subsequent change of
heart. So having abandoned the protection—or, perhaps, the illusion—of traditional institutions, we were forced back to our own
counsel. How could we control the future? We accepted the paradox; we made the one decision that married couples in this age
of do-it-yourself divorce hesitate to make. We agreed that during
the time our child was a dependent person, neither of us would
view separation as an acceptable solution to any problem. It would
be literally unthinkable. And we reached this decision not by exchanging sacred vows or by drafting elaborate legal documents.
We simply said it, knew it.

The coming of parenthood, even the second time around,

brought a multitude of unexpected pressures. Because Alice was over thirty-five (no one even asked my age!), she qualified for the amniocentesis test to ascertain whether the baby suffered chromosomal defects associated with older parents, particularly Down's syndrome. It's one way modern medicine makes it easier for such parents to have healthy babies. But, at bottom, it's a political issue, too, for a negative result on the amniocentesis is meaningless unless the parent is also prepared to have an abortion and, perhaps, try again. During Alice's amnio procedure, I studied the sonogram screen, watched my baby cavort and tumble, dance and spin, and like any proud papa, I started to take photographs of her first performance. I didn't get very far. The mystery froze my fingers. Here was Alice on the table, mildly swollen; and inches away, big as a fish, was our next of kin. Then we had to wait six weeks for the results.

Once that was settled, Alice announced that she expected me to help with the labor. When my son was born in 1969, fathers were strictly forbidden from entering the labor rooms, which, with my propensity to swoon at the thought of blood, suited me fine. Now, in the new climate of the 1980s, the age of shared parenting, my private anxieties carried no clout. Alice dragged me to a series of natural childbirth classes, where we saw movies about animal births and bonding in lambs and zebras; watched other couples drive to the hospital and exit triumphantly; and learned to count our pants and breaths.

Surrounded by equally dumb and frightened men, I gained confidence in my ability—if not to help, at least not to faint. But when the time came, I must confess that I performed fairly well. In fact, because of an unplanned caesarian—a not uncommon occurrence these days, especially among "elderly primaparas," as they coyly call first mothers over the age of thirty-five—our daughter bonded with me. I doubt seriously if it will do her any good, but that first meeting of our eyes remains the most miraculous experience of my life.

What she represented, this bawling girl in my arms, was not just a link to the future, the symbolic immortality that psychologists assure us all people desire. She also howled in defense of her parents. Within this new person, Alice and I had woven together our genetic essence, the sticky glue of the universe, woven it inextricably, perhaps forever. Who, now, could presume to challenge the validity of our relationship?

In this child, I realized, I'd also made another kind of commitment to the future—not just because I'd promised to stay with her mother come hell or high water; not just because this infant evoked my paternal nurturance. But also she aroused a sublime curiosity. Would it matter to her, as it mattered so much to us, that her parents lived beyond the safety of formal institutions? Would she appreciate, and perhaps be inspired by, the essential precariousness that characterizes our lives? Would she also come to know—*what distinguishes our relationship is that we always know* —that despite our most earnest promises, we can still change our minds? Will she understand that we are always beginning again?

Fifteen years after it all began, Alice and I still feel like social outlaws, but I confess we're looking more respectable than ever. In our California suburb we run a typical two-paycheck household and spend an inordinate amount of time balancing our careers with child care. To the neighbors we've become just another family. The year our baby was born, we qualified for the first time for the annual block party: And we went and had a good time.

We seem, in the long view, to have created a nice bit of history between us. But it's a history based less on the crusty cake of custom than on the porous fibers of the uncertainty principle. Appearances notwithstanding, we cling to each other with the fear —and the trust—of acrobats working the high wire. Any day, we may fall. Meanwhile, we luxuriate in the defiance and the dare. For who ever knows when or how it will end?

THIRTEEN

Take Your Time

O utside academia the market for history was not what I expected. While American scholars debated the merits of the new history and clamored after monographs, the literate public was awash in historical romance, typified by the pulp best-sellers of John Jakes's *Kent Family Chronicles,* whose sales approached 50 million copies. As for the nonliterate, the relevant trend was "nostalgia." The fashion industry, ever attuned to sartorial obsolescence, offered first the "Gatsby" look of the 1920s, and moved on to "midis" that evoked the 1930s, before settling on styles of the 1940s and 1950s. Hollywood presented the sepia tones of *Butch Cassidy and the Sundance Kid,* the black and white of *The Last Picture Show,* sentimental glimpses of the Great Depression (*Paper Moon*), and an endless array of grade B movies about the 1950s. Trivia contests, television reruns, and the revival of formica-top tables used a popular interest in the past to deflect interest from what was happening in the present.

The politically mandated Bicentennial of 1976 accelerated the trend. In celebrating Jefferson's Declaration of Independence, the key phrase was "pursuit of happiness." My neighbors in Belmont, California, went around painting the fire hydrants to look like stunted Revolutionary War characters, just one of over sixty thousand community projects around the land that paid homage to the past. Six months later, during a bitter cold spell that froze the nation indoors, ABC's version of "Roots" captured the largest television audience in history. Over 130 million people, more than half the population of the United States, watched at least one segment of the miniseries. Oral history became the rage, as if the past was something to eat, and ironically it stimulated a taste for old regional recipes to make it more palatable!

Here, surely, was ample proof of what I desired: a mass audience for History. But thanks to mass marketing, History had become pleasure—nothing more. Linked exclusively to the satisfactions of the present, it no longer stretched into the past for comparison and contrast. The old ways, in this light, appeared quaint rather than critical, and the present seemed not only logical, the result of Progress, but inevitable and therefore unchangeable. Any lingering unpleasantness—race, class, or war—could conveniently be blamed on the past or, more frequently, simply ignored.

As I searched for my niche as a popular historian, I had to question my precocious retirement. So did my parents. To leave a job with a good pension quickened the never-quite-dormant anxieties of the depression. When I tried to explain my frustrations with the academic professionals, my mother wanted to know who, if not them, had made me so smart! But my parents' worries for me merely revealed their own deeper dreads: the inescapable facts of age. They did not attempt to hide them. "They didn't puff themselves up or fight against it and brag that they weren't going to die," wrote Alexander Solzhenitsyn of the Russian peasants from whom my parents were descended, "they took death *calmly.*
. . . And they departed easily, as if they were just moving into a new house."

As I pondered this gentle phrase, my parents announced out of the blue that they had decided to move. The neighborhood had changed. One night, a gang of teenagers surrounded my father on a dark street, threatening and terrifying him. He, who took such pride in riding at the back of the segregated buses in Biloxi, Mississippi, during World War II and who defied the platitudes of suburbia by insisting we live in a racially mixed neighborhood, now felt betrayed by the climate of racial tension. So they would close down the old house; and with it, I saw, what were undeniably the best years of their lives. Their move now made my earlier departures forever final; there would be no home to return to.

In the summer of 1976, just a few weeks after Jimmy Carter accepted the Democratic nomination at Madison Square Garden, I flew to New York City to help them pack twenty years' accumulations into supermarket cartons for a move deeper into the suburbs. They seemed utterly unprepared for the enormity of the task—and oddly immobilized. Gladly they let me take charge of the disassembling and debolting. In my unsubtle ways I managed to drop and damage. Yet no one seemed to notice or cared to complain, and an uncomfortable calm followed each box down the stairs and into the driveway. Amid the chaos, my mother might flip on her TV show or my father disappear for a quick nap.

"I've been thinking," my mother remarked one morning. "I don't think we'll live in the new house as long as we've lived here."

"I'll take two years," my father replied, knowing he had even less.

From such joyful conversation I was lured by my strawberry-blonde cousin, who insisted we go out for air. On a warm, unhumid Saturday in early September, we headed for Greenwich Village. Maybe it was the perfect weather or just the friendly buzz that surrounded the annual sidewalk art show, but the atmosphere was balmy and mellow, without a trace of urban paranoia. A billow of marijuana washed the air; people smiled at strangers. The Waverly Theater on Sixth Avenue was playing Bergman's *Face to Face*. My cousin bought the *Village Voice* and scanned the local listings; I pocketed the latest *New York* magazine, which advertised a piece by Tom Wolfe. Then we headed north on Sixth, stopping outside a caged schoolyard to watch some street athletes play full-court basketball.

"Is it coincidental," she asked, "that these city kids are so terrific at a game of feints and sneaks and quick runs?"

The scream of a siren stopped my response: A racing ambulance, heading north up Sixth, abruptly broke out of the traffic and

pulled to the curb, its siren choking strangely—"whoo," "whoo"—
like a tired locomotive. The white-uniformed driver stepped into
the street and rushed to the double doors at the back.

"Take your time," called the round-bellied policeman who
greeted him at the curb. "He's only an OD."

The cop pointed with his stick to a bareheaded black man, probably in his twenties, who was sprawled across a cement-and-wood
park bench. His head inclined backward, resting against the top
rung. His long body stretched out straight, ending in a pair of
black-and-white basketball sneakers tied with iridescent purple
laces. As my cousin and I watched, the paramedics and policeman
coolly went about their business: checking for the heartbeat; finding a black rubber sheath and some needles; dropping a starched
green hospital sheet on the grimacing face; filling out forms; at
last, wheeling the corpse into the ambulance.

"Take your time," my cousin murmured. "Did you hear what
that cop said?"

"I can't believe he said it," I replied.

"I can believe it," she declared. "I can't believe he said it so
loud."

Later that day, as I rested in my old bed for the last time, I un-
rolled the *New York* magazine and read about the "Me Decade."
Tom Wolfe, grinning in his white suit, had discovered the Third
Great Awakening—a chic, hedonistic search for the perfect self—
personified, as he described it, by a rich blonde woman from Los
Angeles pinpointing the vortex of her delight. Consumer capitalism had reached a new plateau: The pursuit of pleasure had
acquired cult status. In this year of the Bicentennial, America
was indeed the land of the new masses. He mentioned a New
York Knickerbocker basketball star who would forever wear Ban-
lon instead of the old blue collar. "The word *proletarian* can no
longer be used in this country with a straight face," said Wolfe
with a straight face.

(Did that, I wondered, explain the purple shoelaces?)

Wolfe, as ever, had his finger on the national pulse. Two
weeks after the article appeared, *Newsweek*'s cover story, "Getting

Your Head Together," heralded a new "consciousness revolution," which was described as a "culturally pervasive movement that may well turn out to be this century's version of colonial America's Great Awakening." Listing the latest fare in America's spiritual cafeteria—Rolfing, psychosynthesis, bioenergetics, guided fantasy, Arica, biofeedback, Silva Mind Control, Feldenkreis—the magazine optimistically suggested that the movement could "put seekers progressively in touch with themselves, with others, with nature and—at its most ambitious—with the fundamental forces of the cosmos."

(The article, I noted, did not mention the traditional sports, such as basketball.)

Ellen Goodman, in a syndicated column that same month, expressed a similar conviction: "we have turned inward, to the search for personal solutions. . . . This self-centering is not only a retreat from the world, but a by-product of the current condition of our lives."

Two weeks later, historian Christopher Lasch published "The Narcissist Society" in the *New York Review of Books*. "The retreat to purely personal satisfactions—such as they are—is one of the main themes of the Seventies," he declared. "Having no hope of improving their lives in any ways that matter, people have convinced themselves that what matters is psychic self-improvement."

Thus in a mere five weeks was born another cliché: the narcissistic seventies. The idea satisfied a popular penchant for dividing history into decades. And by juxtaposing adjectives (silent fifties, tumultuous sixties, sleepy seventies), it reduced historical change to a cyclical series of oedipal jousts, one generation rejecting its predecessors, which rejected its predecessors . . . and so on back to the Gay Nineties. But were these adjectives true? Whose history was this, anyway?

There is little doubt that Wolfe, Lasch, Goodman, et al. were describing a reality they had experienced and understood. How many divorces they had observed! How many trips to the therapist! How much witless news commentary! How many commercials! But to me, their collective wisdom boiled down to an aphorism, written by the nineteenth-century pedagogue William McGuffey in a story entitled "The Poor Boy": "The rich have many troubles which we know nothing of."

The dead man with the purple shoelaces evoked a different reality, albeit less glamorous, than that of the blonde from Los Angeles. Yet the rapid acceptance of the "Me Decade" as a shorthand description of the seventies made it extremely awkward to approach his world. The sophisticated writers not only ignored the problems of the poor, such as drug abuse, but also trivialized their condition. After all, to understand the predicament of the disadvantaged one might really have to confront the word *proletarian* with a straight face. But the notion of the Me Decade offered a crippling logic: "After the political turmoil of the sixties," wrote Lasch, "Americans have retreated to purely personal preoccupations." Just as the "turbulent" sixties ignored my generation of liberals (not to mention moderates and conservatives), the invention of the narcissistic seventies eliminated more current styles of deviance and dissent. By definition, political controversy, social protest, now belonged to the past. To speak otherwise implied some obstinate anachronism.

As I probed deeper I discovered that the depreciation of the seventies had its own curious, Orwellian history. It began, interestingly, with President Nixon, a man preoccupied with his place on the national pedestal. Although the early years of his administration provoked numerous examples of "sixties" behavior—the opposition to the Cambodia "incursion" that led to the shootings at Kent State University, the May Day demonstrations of 1971, the Attica uprising, the occupation of Alcatraz Island, the siege at Wounded Knee, to name the most famous incidents—the president frequently used the fiction of discrete decades (the sixties versus the seventies) to place political dissent safely behind him, in the past, in the age of LBJ. "It is easy to forget how frightful it was," said the Republicans in the past tense (in 1972). "There was Vietnam—so bloody, so costly, so bitterly divisive. . . . At home our horrified people watched our cities burn, crime burgeon, cam-

puses dissolve into chaos." The ahistorical solution: Four More
Years. After Watergate and the final failure in Vietnam, the Ford
administration recommended a similar politics of amnesia: "Concentrate on problems of the future," advised Henry Kissinger. In
the presidential election of 1976, Jimmy Carter refused—on principle!—to discuss the war or even Watergate. No wonder, then,
that the narcissist writings of the summer of 1976 were so rapidly
embraced!

Surely we should hesitate to blame the messenger for the bad
tidings. In this case, though, the media, the reporters and the
culture critics, were not just couriers of information. They created the vocabulary within which any discourse could occur.
They controlled the realm of the possible. And because they
claimed a certain political neutrality—the objective observer in
the television booth, the academic in the cloister—their commentary possessed an inordinate influence, a respect no longer given
freely to professional politicians. In the seventies the intellectuals
betrayed that trust. The Me Decade became the standard against
which "normal" behavior would be measured.

My father never had to contend with the cult of narcissism. He
would have hated the phrase, seeing in its psychological elegance
a cold disdain for the troubles of ordinary people. He had too
much respect for the limits of time: He understood that the historical moment frames the available options. It was gratuitous to
condemn powerless people for failing to exercise power over their
lives; it was dishonest to condemn them when their efforts to do
so did not succeed. He liked to remind me that some people had
to work for a living. But coincidental with the invention of the Me
Decade, my father suddenly died of an aneurism.

Soon after, I returned to California to launch my own study of
contemporary history. Rather quickly I found myself grappling
with a peculiarly American sense of time. Despite the popular
interest in historical subjects, no one seems to know—or care
—when anything happened (much less why). To talk about the
founding of America, for example, is to mouth hated school les-

sons or the shibboleths of mistrusted politicians. Clio, the muse of history, languishes in a back room, seldom summoned, barely understood. The living history sleeps.

Yet the desire for historical connection endures. Perhaps it is an essential human need, something tied to the species, this urge to live in time, to hold a sense of the past as well as a hope for the future. For History provides the ballast in the quest for immortality; it links us to tradition. And if that need is there, so is its solution, even if the product is culturally conditioned, adulterated, prepackaged, and sold. This much is true. As a people we are preoccupied by dates and anniversaries. The mass media are forever presenting flashbacks: packaged nostalgia, historical romance, reruns.

In recent years we have bred an entire industry of calendars, each offering preprinted reminders of the past. Here trivia abounds: In *The Liberated Woman's Appointment Calendar: 1974* —the year I quit academia—I find (randomly turning the pages) that on January 8 "Sarah Carmichael Harrell, first female teacher to receive pay equal with male teachers in southeast Indiana, born, 1844," or for June 9 that "Sophie Hume, famed Quaker preacher, arrives in Charleston, S.C., from London for a highly acclaimed visit and speaking tour, 1767." What marvelous details! Imagine what they'll be saying about us in two hundred years. Then, I wonder, why can't we say it about ourselves right now?

To see our times as historical defies the conventional wisdom that we lack "a proper perspective"—as if total strangers, yet unborn, may know us better than we know ourselves. Given all our insights into the cultural blindness of historians, can we reasonably expect an "objective" rendering of the last decades of the twentieth century? In any event, the historical report card will come too late to do us any good. Meanwhile, in the absence of a historical sensibility, we leave the territory to pundits and politicians who look at our times with neither objectivity nor hindsight.

We surrender in this way not only the advantages of historical wisdom but also its power. We allow others, like the narcissists, to define our times, to establish agendas, even to deny the relevance of precedent and history altogether. And the habit lingers.

The idea that the age of Reagan represented a "new" time, a distinct era, for example, had enduring political consequences. Public events—the embargo on Iran, the bombing of Libya, the war in Nicaragua—emerged one by one as separate issues, unrelated to each other and to our common history. It took a major scandal—Contragate—to bring the connections into the public view. And still we were forced to rely on "expert" commentators to unravel what it all meant. To live in history, by contrast, provides coherence. It offers the power to understand, and perhaps even to change, the course of time.

FOURTEEN

History Lost

Working for no one was to work for anyone. As a "free-lance" historian, I found no assignment beneath my dig-nity. I wrote articles about electric vibrators and strip-tease dancers; preached to the local Congregationalists about American landscapes; "consulted" with textbook publishers about marketing strategies; and created a dog-and-pony show for the campus lecture circuit. I even returned to the classroom, teaching part time at night for a pittance and none of the old perquisites. I was grateful for a subsistence.

Scrambling after an income was new and not wholly unplea-surable. The advantages of self-employment were obvious: no shoes, no ties, no cold-morning shaves. There were also prin-ciples involved, part of the postcounterculture philosophy of self-reliance and minimal obligations to the corporate world. Such virtues suited the times. When the Arab oil embargo produced those horrendous gasoline lines, I had the privilege of walking to work in the next room. After the ensuing recession took away Alice's job, she too set up her writing shop at home. Without romanticizing the unexpected poverty, we enjoyed a pride in self-sufficiency and tried quite deliberately to blur the lines between private satisfactions and our work. Reading and book reviewing became interchangeable activities, and my passion for the movies quickly developed into an area of expertise for which I could be paid.

Good history remained my objective, by which I meant a history that reflected my values and overall worldview. I saw the task as pedagogical. In my most grandiose imagination I wished to inculcate the lessons of the new history to a vast American classroom. Any means—a pithy review, a speech, a letter to the editor—could serve that end. For I believed that a knowledge of the past was crucial for building a sense of empowerment among ordinary citizens. Only by stripping away the stereotypes and icons of Americana, the familiar liturgy that led inexorably from Jamestown and the Mayflower Compact to Nixon, Ford, and Carter, could people see their own times as a function of history, which is to say the result of human choice and the exercise of power. History, in this view, would illuminate the past not for its own sake but to reflect upon ourselves and, ultimately, to goad a free people into action. As with the Puritans of yore, such a missionary zeal justified certain material sacrifices.

It was in this spirit that I opened myself to the history around me. In northern California, where I moved when I was thirty, I identified an older generation of exiles whose political attitudes were similar to mine and who appreciated the need for a relevant history. Some had migrated from Los Angeles and Hollywood when the blacklisting of the 1950s deprived them of income and friends. Some had come to San Francisco and Berkeley in the 1960s with the same fervor that earlier had taken them to Spain and Normandy and Cuba. Some, as they aged, preferred the milder winters. Together they embodied a living history—not anachronism but a profound sense of the past and a yearning to extend it in time.

It was my love of Spain that brought me to them.

In 1975 Alvah Bessie, one of the last survivors of the blacklisted Hollywood 10, published a book about Franco's Spain—a subject about which I knew a thing or two—and Francis Coppola's soon-to-be-defunct *City* magazine sent me to interview him. Bessie's career had seen a remarkable cycle of ups and downs—acclaim as a story writer, battlefields in Spain, an Oscar nomination as a screenwriter, a year in federal prison, huge income followed by total unemployment, three marriages, three children, a mix of adoration and betrayal—but through it all, I would discover, there remained one constant theme: He was a grouch, a lovable grouch; even when he was nice, he was gruff.

A decade older than most of the veterans of the Lincoln Battalion, Bessie was seventy and living in involuntary retirement in suburban Marin County north of the Golden Gate Bridge. He met me at the front door, shook hands firmly, and shouted hello —the result of a hearing loss caused by bombardments in Spain in 1938. A red polo shirt offset his round, bald head, giving an immediate impression of health and strength. He looked like one tough geezer. Then he led me through the tidy rooms and outside again into his backyard wherein existed the ultimate luxury of seven decades of revolutionary idealism: a swimming pool about which he was understandably proud. He suggested we go skinny-dipping. When I declined, he offered me a drink.

"Do you have beer?"

"What's wrong with gin and tonic?" He articulated each word with the diction of an actor. "Dalton Trumbo always said that was the only decent drink."

Tradition was tradition. He returned with two gin and tonics. "Now what do you want with an old shit like me?" he growled.

I was interested in his recent return to Barcelona and proceeded with my interview questions, which he answered fondly and loudly, his lidded eyes misting as the sun rose and he recalled comrades buried in Spain. It was clear that their deaths still haunted him, obliging him to continue their common struggle against Spanish fascism. He showed me the draft of a public letter he had just composed protesting the execution of so-called Basque terrorists. It was addressed to "El Puto."

"Do you know what a puta is?" he asked.

I could barely count to ten in Spanish. But once in New York there had been a Puerto Rican kid in my class, and that was his favorite word. I shook my head.

"Franco is a puta." Bessie drained the melted ice from his glass. "But he will die soon. Then it will have been worth the wait."

We talked amicably through the afternoon—Bessie was a superb raconteur—and at the end of the interview he invited me to a private screening of a film about the Spanish civil war made by one of his former comrades in the Abraham Lincoln Battalion. Bessie could not attend, but he gave me directions to an elegant home in the Berkeley hills with a vista that pulled the eye toward China. The woman who greeted me at the door might well have played mah-jongg with my mother in the Bronx. She was slightly built, friendly but shy, and she had used the faintest daub of red rouge to brighten an otherwise grayish pallor. She led me into an uncarpeted living room. The furniture had been pushed against the walls to make room for a dozen folding chairs that faced a collapsible screen. Three or four older couples had occupied the nearest seats, but my host neglected to make introductions. After a while I concluded that eye contact was no longer in vogue among old revolutionaries. Nor did I see any of the candy dishes my mother surely would have assembled for such an important social occasion. Luckily, the other chairs soon filled with gray-headed guests, and the film, *Dreams and Nightmares,* unfolded quickly on the small screen.

Abe Osheroff, a carpenter by trade, had made the autobiographical movie to explain his continuing involvement with the Left. Unemployed during the depression and a Jew, he had volunteered to fight fascism in Spain, enjoying brief moments of glory until he was wounded at Belchite. He described the defeat of the Republic and the subsequent betrayal of Spain by the Allies after World War II. The story climaxed thirty years later with his decision to return to Spain—to reaffirm his earlier sacrifice and to continue the fight against Franco's dictatorship. It was a moving testament, distinguished not so much by its politics as by the unvarnished depiction of one man's personal commitment, his understated passion for social justice. I would learn later that Osheroff had been a political fugitive in the 1950s, surfacing in the next decade as a civil rights worker in Mississippi. In the

1980s he would go off to Nicaragua and build thirty private homes for the campesinos.

When the movie ended, a stunning woman of about sixty, identified only as Frieda, told us confidentially about recent communications smuggled out of Spain from underground dissidents— union leaders, priests, former prisoners of the regime—and she exhorted us about the importance of preventing the ratification of a pending mutual defense treaty between Spain and the United States, which would provide modern weapons to the dictatorship. She spoke eloquently despite the low-keyed surroundings. Her blue eyes shimmered and her voice rose; her fine white hair seemed luminescent. She was a skilled orator, mingling pathetic stories of arrest and torture with a crisp rage at the men who made American foreign policy. Then she called for donations, and I gave gladly much more than I could afford.

Forty years earlier my parents had been among these people. But long before I developed my own political conscience, they had abandoned the faith. As I listened to Frieda that night, I knew that my mother would have been put off by her fluency, and my father would have lamented the futility of her pleas. Maybe that is why I was so generous. For among these believers I felt embarrassed about my parents, a shame for their lack of persistence. As I was growing up they would never even discuss this part of their past. It constituted one of those dreams that had died with the war. I was a teenager before I learned I was a red-diaper baby; only then did I understand why as a child I'd been sung to sleep by Paul Robeson's Russian lullabies. Fear had silenced their politics —HUAC and all that. So had the beckoning postwar prosperity. When my father became a public-school teacher in 1947, it was his first steady job, loyalty oath or no. Perhaps too—this, at least, I like to think—they could not sustain the omnipresent anger, Frieda's daily rage, necessary for the revolutionary foot soldier.

Before I left, I added my name to the mailing list, and a few months later I received an invitation to the annual reunion of the Lincoln Battalion, at which Alvah Bessie was to be honored. On a miserable, rainy Sunday afternoon, I drove across the Bay Bridge to a landmark seafood restaurant in Berkeley. Because of my late arrival, I discovered I could not be seated in the main dining hall, which accommodated some four hundred people. Since the spillover included Governor Jerry Brown, it was not exactly an insult, or at least not an obvious one, the Old Left being somewhat unimpressed with Emily Post. But sitting opposite me at the table of exiles was the wife of a Lincoln veteran, a stunning Swedish woman named Anna. She was wearing a handwoven white lace blouse and silver pendant, and her eyes were the reason someone had invented the word blue. Despite age, wrinkles, and an arthritic stiffness, Anna was beautiful. And attentive; she felt responsible for the second-rate treatment I'd received. When she learned I was a historian, she promised to introduce me to the most interesting man in the hall, who happened to be her husband.

He was at that moment standing behind the room-length bar, decanting gallon jugs of red wine into unlabeled green bottles. Anna drew me across the room to meet him just as Alvah Bessie began to speak. "I'm Red," announced the ruddy, round-faced man, extending a muscular hand that failed somehow to grasp my own. He pointed to his snow-white hair. "Red," he repeated with a rich and bubbling laugh. "Not 'a Red.' They used to call me the Red Rooster." He pushed an empty glass across the bar and then a full bottle.

In the months since I'd interviewed Bessie, El Puto had died, and the old radicals were celebrating his departure. With Bessie's voice in the background, Red and I toasted each other and then listened to the familiar indictment of United States policy toward Spain for the past forty years. Perhaps because the acoustics were so bad and we were so far from the dais, the speech seemed endless. We drank another glass of red wine and a third. Red put a match to his corncob pipe and cast a cloud of blue smoke between us. "Next year," Bessie was concluding, "in Madrid!" The huge audience abruptly rose in applause. But I noticed Red was not clapping. "Some of my comrades," he said, leaning over the bar, "never got over Spain."

I was surprised by the pronouncement and then by his candor. What did he mean? "These people here are great people," he said, sweeping the room with mirthful blue eyes. "The very best. Salt of the earth and all. But God damn it, you can't live in the fucking past for forty years."

Red wanted to know what I did, and when I explained that I wrote about American history, his face brightened. "I guess I've seen a fair bit myself." He looked me straight in the eye. "You know, there are rumors that some of us may not be around forever."

Would he tell me his story? We arranged to meet at his house in San Francisco one evening after work. Red was a shop steward at a cannery that specialized in mayonnaise. He had worked on the line for almost twenty years—often on swing shift for the extra pay. His awkward handshake, I later learned, was the result of an industrial accident that severed the tendons in his hand. He was well-educated, too, and loved to read. Over the years he had discovered places in the factory to hide out with a good book. His small library consequently comprised the dirtiest books I had ever seen—literally dirty, with greasy fingerprint smudges on almost every page. "There are some things I know," he promised, "that might interest you."

Red ladled beef stew from an iron pot into three Mexican ceramic plates, and I set up the tape recorder at the center of the round wooden table in the kitchen. Anna came out to say hello. She was shy about the recorder, however, and whispered discreetly when it was on. So her voice lives now only as a muffled disruption. Anyway, she assured me, she had heard enough of her husband's narrative and just wanted to make sure that I got it straight. Her story, she insisted, had no importance. Then she took her plate and disappeared into another room.

I started by beating the bushes for war stories, and Red laughingly described his most memorable experience as the time he chauffered a young lieutenant right through the plate-glass window of a downtown pharmacy in Indianapolis, Indiana, thereby accelerating his transfer into the infantry in 1942. He'd been drafted before Pearl Harbor, but only after he was rejected by both the marines and the army because of his political background.

Like other "premature antifascists," as the military called the American veterans of the Spanish civil war, he'd been classified as a potential subversive. Soon after his induction, he was ordered to Camp Riley in Little Falls, Minnesota, not too far from the hometown of Charles Lindbergh, who was then in the headlines for opposing United States intervention in the war against Germany. The first night there Red was taking a shower with another man "suspected of disloyalty." The fellow spoke conspiratorially: "I'm worried about what's happening at Stalingrad."

"What do you mean?" Red wondered.

"We had such an easy time in Paris," answered the American Nazi, whereupon Red turned on the hot water full blast. When the MPs arrived, Red was sitting on the guy's chest.

"This son of a bitch is a Nazi," Red reported.

"You should talk," countered the sergeant; "you're a goddamn Communist!"

How had he become a Communist?

"In a Roman Catholic school," he said with an ex–altar boy's glee. As a teenager, he had naïvely asked a social studies teacher to explain the existence of so much unemployment in America. "People in the neighborhood are going hungry and you're teaching epistemology." The teacher replied by sending him to the principal's office, where Red was asked to repeat his question. The principal then wanted to know if he was a Communist. "I'd never heard the term before," said Red, "but I decided right then to find out what the hell it is."

Did he know about Spain before he volunteered in 1937?

"I knew nothing about Spain," he said earnestly. But he had seen a movie newsreel of a crying Jew in Vienna who was being forced to scrub the sidewalk with a toothbrush while a bunch of brownshirts stood around laughing. "If these motherfuckers are going to take over a continent," Red recalled his feelings, "this isn't a world I can live in." But because of his Irish Catholic background, the Communist party was slow to process his papers!

I turned the conversation toward the question of survivorship, the psychological burden of war that seemed to be haunting Alvah Bessie. Red thought Bessie would have felt different if he'd gotten into World War II; as it was, he said, "Spain was the most vivid thing in his life." Having fought in both wars, Red had seen so much death, experiencing victory as well as defeat, that he held a fatalistic view of his survival. The word he preferred was "luck," and he used it often. As an example, he told about being assigned to an exposed machine-gun nest in Spain and being ordered to take a mule to get some food. Under cover of darkness, he led the mule through heavy artillery fire, found supplies in a nearby town, lashed the material to the mule, and returned through more artillery fire only to find that the outpost had received a direct hit and everyone was dead.

Did he ever feel the guilt we heard so much about when speaking of Vietnam veterans?

Red's brother, a Jesuit priest, had been an army chaplain in Vietnam, and he had described the personal traumas of that war. Nothing similar had occurred in Spain, said Red. He had never heard a single veteran of that war ever mention anything he was ashamed of "apart from the lack of bravery." And in World War II he had personally witnessed several examples of American soldiers refusing to follow orders that would have resulted in the death of Italian civilians. In a company composed of ordinary infantrymen—"not politicals," Red emphasized—the American colonel could not get his men to clear civilians from the road leading to Palermo. "He just lost his command."

To Red, then, Vietnam was a "terrible turnaround," with the soldiers victimized by their own ideology. "They accept the verdict of history that this was an unjust war," he said, apologizing for the use of a Catholic term, "an abomination in their own experience." He felt sorry for those soldiers. But not so sorry that he didn't want to see an honest reckoning. He proposed a Nuremburg-type tribunal with the winners of the war dragging the enemy leaders—Nixon, McNamara, Kissinger—into court. He wasn't being funny. It was a matter of justice. It would soothe a lot of guilty consciences.

Anna was right. Her husband would be the most interesting Lincoln brigadier I met. He was simply brilliant—ironic, profound, and compassionate. By the time the tape recorder clicked off, we were getting along so well that it seemed a mistake to break the mood. I decided not to change the cassette. Anna peeked in around midnight to say goodnight and assumed we were hard at work. The next day I scribbled some notes and invented more questions to ask. But later, after we all became close friends, the tape recorder seemed an artificial excuse to get together. I thought there would be plenty of time to get Red's story preserved for posterity. Then, one lovely afternoon in June, he died of a heart attack.

I felt both proud and foolish that the only tangible thing I ever got to keep was that first hour in which Red talked about survivals and Vietnam and Nuremberg. So much of his remarkable saga— Spain, the concentration camps, the communist underground— these episodes endure only in my memory. I carry Red's stories carefully.

About such precious information the poet Czeslow Milosz says: "And this is what haunted me in those years I lived after you; a question: Where is the truth of unmentioned things?"

FIFTEEN

History Found

As Red's life slipped into the past, I knew I had failed him, indeed, had neglected my craft. Having asked for his intimacy, having taken it, I had squandered the inheritance. So much human effort strives for immortality, but only the existence of a sympathetic recipient—a descendant, a survivor, a curious passerby who pauses to pick up the traces—can give the power of transcendence. Kill the empathetic future, that urge for preservation, and whole lifetimes may vanish like a species extinct.

Could I keep Red alive? Could I salvage the spirit he represented—the engaged intellectual, the university graduate who fought in foreign wars, who organized mine workers in Montana, who spent his last twenty years in a mayonnaise factory, eschewing promotions so that minority workers could get ahead? Could I capture his wit, his humility, his sense of irony? These I wanted not for myself (for I held them inside) but for an indefinite posterity, appreciative though remote. I could only try.

I began at his funeral, an event Red himself nearly missed. He had died while on vacation with Anna in the high Sierra, and she decided to have the body cremated on the spot. She returned to San Francisco to charter a fishing boat for a scattering-of-the-ashes ceremony outside the Golden Gate. Red had loved to fish the Pacific waters for salmon, and he left behind several dozen cans of the smoked fish. Anna planned to serve them to the small group of friends and family who would pay their respects. While she made these arrangements, the crematory packaged Red's remains in a small legal-sized box—the kind of marble-colored cardboard container you often see on a lawyer's shelf—and gave it into the custody of the federal government, specifically the U.S. Postal Service. Once there, it disappeared.

As Red's friends converged in Sausalito on a warm July afternoon, Anna made her own preparations by burning the *San Francisco Chronicle* and sifting its remains through a kitchen strainer to create the proper dusty look. Why she went to all the trouble became apparent when I met Red's brother, the Vietnam War priest, known as Father Bill. He was taller than Red, a puffed-up version, in the way resemblances run in a family. In the heat he stripped to the waist, revealing a muscular, hairless torso. Regardless of Red's religious principles, or total lack thereof, Father Bill had come to officiate. He insisted, in good jesuitical fashion, that Red had never really departed from the true faith. "Measured by the standard of caring for others," he declared most earnestly, Red was "as religious as any person I have ever known." Even a strident atheist could not resist that logic.

Father Bill announced he would read from the military service for those buried at sea. It seemed as appropriate as any. Red had proven himself a tough soldier. Besides Spain, he had fought through North Africa, Sicily, Italy, France, and Germany and came out without a scratch. He had hit the beach at Anzio, the only man in his elite amphibious unit to escape injury, and had earned a Silver Star for courage under fire. Anyway, a military funeral seemed sufficiently nondenominational for a lapsed Communist.

As the little fishing boat thumped against the tide, Jonesy, one of Red's pals from the Lincoln Battalion, regaled us with Red's latest ruminations about religion. "He used to affect a thick Irish brogue," Jonesy recalled. "The other night, as he was hanging up the phone, he said in this deep Irish voice, 'And may God keep and preserve you.'

"'Red,' I said, 'I thought you were an atheist.'

" 'I am, my boy. But I've no faith in it!' "

When the boat got about a mile beyond the bridge, Father Bill summoned us to the stern, made his short sermon about the faith of soldiers, and then shook the dusty contents of the lawyer's box into the green sea. Anna gave each of us freshly picked flowers from her garden—mine were the saffron and yellow colors of Spain—and we threw our garlands, one by one, into a widening pool of ash. Anna waited a moment. Then she dropped a single yellow rose into the wake.

As the boat headed back to shore, Red's youngest brother, a distinguished professor at a prominent university, reminisced about their childhood in the Pacific Northwest. He was a slender man, thinner in the cheeks than his brothers. Accompanied by his wife and young son, he appeared rather professorial in his wool tweed jacket. Except that the sleeve was now lightly flecked with the residue of Red's ashes. (Or was it the *Chronicle*? Anna later swore that Red had indeed arrived that morning, but she, also an atheist, could never entirely convince me by all her subsequent oaths.) Professor Sam, in any case, was oblivious to the white dust on his tweed jacket.

Fifteen years younger than Red, Professor Sam relied less on memory than on the verities of family tradition. Their parents were Irish immigrants, quite poor and very Catholic. His father worked for the railroad. When the Great Depression hit, they became poorer. One Friday afternoon, Red's pious mother made a thick soup from the marrow bones brought by a charitable priest. Red, then about sixteen, returned from school, peeked inside the pot, and asked with a straight face whether it might perhaps be hypocritical for a Catholic woman to be using meat bones on a Friday. His mother lifted the iron ladle and bopped him on his red head.

He repeated the story of Red's political awakening—the principal who accused him of communism; the Movietone newsreel showing the Jew in Vienna; Red's decision to leave college to enlist for Spain. He was twenty-one. But he hesitated to tell the family; good Catholics, they supported Franco and would have seen their son arrested first. So he announced instead that he'd gotten a job on a French newspaper, and off he went down the communist pipeline and across the Pyrenees. Red tried to maintain the fiction, writing only to his sister from "France," but, of course, the postmarks gave him away. His mother, convinced that her oldest son was murdering priests and raping nuns, promptly went to bed—and stayed there for over a year.

Professor Sam remembered Red chatting in the kitchen about the Spanish war. But Anna offered a different version. When Red returned from the war, his oldest sister was sent to meet him at the railroad station. "You might as well stay on the train," she said, summing up the family judgment. And he did.

The tide was running fast, pushing the fishing boat from the stern. Enormous waves leaped like walruses and washed across our shoes. The teenagers, Red's younger children, nieces, and nephews, huddled together on the ship's bridge and sipped brandy. Red's oldest son, for reasons never clearly stated, had not come.

Jonesy picked up on the Anzio story, filling in details. After the bloody battle on the beaches, Red's outfit moved into the hills and began to capture large numbers of German soldiers. The prisoners were disarmed, ordered to remove their shoes, and then escorted down to the coast. Red noticed that one lieutenant completed these trips with remarkable alacrity, and he decided to follow him. In a cluster of trees, he saw the lieutenant standing behind a kneeling prisoner. Bodies of German soldiers lay around him. Red aimed his rifle at the lieutenant. "You know," he later told Jonesy, "I didn't fight my way through Spain, Africa, and Italy to kill prisoners."

"After that, they didn't shoot prisoners?" asked Jonesy.

"I don't know," said Red, "but they didn't shoot them when I was around."

I mentioned Red's reference to another mutiny, when his commanding officer ordered the men to clear the road to Palermo and the GIs had refused. Red had contrasted the experience with the indiscriminate killing in Vietnam. Jonesy said Red also thwarted an artilleryman who was taking target practice with captured mortars at the peasants on a distant hill. Yet a few months later, when Red witnessed the liberation of a German concentration camp, he proposed a simple solution to the problems of denazification: line the SS against the wall and shoot. "There would be no poetry lost," he said.

After the fishing boat docked we all went back to Red and Anna's house. She placed the empty lawyer's box on a cedar chest in the narrow hallway and led us into the kitchen for the smoked salmon and Spanish brandy. Through an open door, I studied the overgrown foliage that blocked any view of the bay. "I don't know what makes me think of it at a time like this," said Anna, interrupting my thoughts. "The morbidity, I suppose. But you know, when they were building the new subway lines down there"—she pointed vaguely beyond the backyard—"we had mice here all the time. One evening I came home from work and there was Red standing on the big table in complete terror. He was terrified of rodents."

She told me why: After the retreat across the Ebro River in 1938, Red had volunteered to swim back under cover of darkness to rescue any survivors. The river had been swollen by the spring thaw, and the water was icy cold. When he reached the shore, Red could hear the fascist soldiers speaking loudly in Spanish, and in the glow of their bonfires he could see the armies of rats feasting on the bodies of his comrades.

"But what the hell," she said. "He was brave about so many other things."

He was tough and nurturant and funny.

A dark-haired woman with sparkling green eyes, young enough to have been Red's daughter, described her last meeting with Red. He had just suffered a heart attack, and she had come to cheer him up. "It may come as a surprise to you," he said, "but some of us revolutionaries are getting old."

"Okay," she said, "but you can still become a millionaire." She told him how: "Take an ad in the *New York Review of Books:* 'Learn the Truth About Mail Fraud.' Tell them to send ten dollars. Then mail back a postcard: 'Consider this a cheap lesson.'

"Learn the truth about capitalism," he'd replied with his great, round-bellied laugh.

Already I was missing Red. He had knit us together for the

last time—his brothers, Jonesy, Anna, the young woman, and me. Each of us cherished an anecdote, an occasion, some personal version of the past. For these few hours our separate memories could intersect to form a history. It was Red's, and now ours, too. But I saw that this was a history consisting of pure desire: the wish to remember.

As I entered the hallway to say goodbye to Anna, I noticed that the lawyer's box had been moved slightly on the cedar chest. Where it had first rested there remained a thin line of white powder that apparently had seeped out from a crack. I was too amazed —horrified—to say anything. Eventually, the line would disintegrate, disappear, and maybe some portion of Red's anatomy would settle into a corner of his house forever.

It confirmed the last thing he said to me, as we departed together from a reunion of the Lincoln Battalion: "I'll be back again next year—as a ghost."

The next day we all gathered again for a proper memorial service at a Unitarian center in Berkeley. The setting was dignified; the speeches more formal. His brother the priest reaffirmed Red's religion; his brother the professor boasted of Red's pedagogical skills. Old soldiers talked about his courage; radicals about his reliability. The wits repeated his jokes. "Cheer up," urged Anna, reciting one of Red's lines, "the worst is yet to come."

Through it all, I knew there was yet another facet to Red's story, less glamorous, less flattering than the others, but nonetheless compatible—a side of his life he had entrusted particularly to me (one that never got into the tape recorder). It spoke to the questions of history, the difference between living in the past and growing from the past, the ability to see one's life as part of an unfolding process. Red took no special pride in the details; quite otherwise, I suspect. He discussed his political activities in fits and starts, spread over months of conversations in our homes, while walking through the San Francisco zoo, at a Giants game at Candlestick Park. He drew no conclusions; he would have been embarrassed at the notion. But it is a good story, full of irony and failure and enduring compassion.

After World War II, Red, like so many other veterans, settled down, got married, and started a family. But unlike most, he stayed in the Communist party, working first in the building trades around San Francisco and then as an organizer among iron miners in the western states. It was bleak and cold there, and he remembered with no small mirth riding alone on an overnight train, the car totally empty save one man sitting opposite him—an FBI agent with whom he shared a bottle of brandy to keep warm. When the Red scare of the 1950s led the CP to establish a secret underground, Red and his wife were among those asked to disappear. They left their young son in the care of a comrade, changed their name to Griffith (after the Irish revolutionary), and took a bus to Los Angeles to preserve the revolution.

Red got a job in a radio factory; his wife, a college-educated professional, became a printer's secretary. They rented a bungalow, bought secondhand furniture, and kept to themselves. They maintained intermittent contact with their son. And except for a single and terribly complicated rendezvous with a "contact," they appeared essentially apolitical—waiting for instructions or a shift in the winds.

Red became aware, nonetheless, of a tail. In those days the FBI purportedly outnumbered the bona fide revolutionaries in the CP underground. (A colleague of mine, who worked briefly for army intelligence, knew of a four-man cell in Nebraska in which three quarters of the membership were federal agents.) In Red's case the prime agent made no effort to disguise his identity. Nor, unlike most of J. Edgar Hoover's employees, did he attempt at that time to harass Red or jeopardize his employment. (That would come later.) In the mornings Red took the bus to work while the agent traveled behind in a black Chevy; in the evenings they reversed the commute. Other people, including, as Red once put it, a remarkably ugly woman with blue eyes and a blond mustache, watched him at night. In this way the game continued for several months, until Red received instructions to return to San Francisco.

It was a welcome change, but the move created additional problems. Red didn't own a car and couldn't afford to buy one. If he traveled by public transportation, it would be expensive. He would have to leave behind personal possessions. Once before the FBI had seized hundreds of his books. It seemed a bit unnecessary.

So the next day Red approached his FBI tail and explained his problem. The agent was not unsympathetic, particularly because his sole task in life was to know all he could about Red's whereabouts. He promised assistance. Within the week he helped Red load all his possessions into an official FBI vehicle and then proceeded to drive Red and his wife four hundred miles through the night to San Francisco.

Not many months later, Nikita Khrushchev presented a speech to the twentieth plenary session of the Communist party in Moscow, denouncing the late Josef Stalin for various crimes against Marx, Lenin, and the Bolshevik revolution. As party members in California debated these revelations, Khrushchev moved Soviet tanks into Budapest to crush the Hungarian uprising. For Red, the betrayals had gone too far. Like thousands of other diehard Communists in 1957, he and his wife resigned their membership in the party.

They tried to create a new life. Red found a job at the cannery, joined the union, and worked steadfastly for the revolution, as he had in Los Angeles, within the capitalist system. They had another child, and then a third. They bought a small house with a big kitchen on the outskirts of San Francisco. They built bookcases and filled them with cheap volumes about Ireland and Spain. Their comrades in the party had to drop them publicly, but many others quit at the same time, and they were able to keep open their lines to the past. They made new friends in the neighborhood; they tried to be normal.

It was too much for his wife. She began to drink, and then to stay away. She eventually abandoned Red, her children, the modest conveniences of security. By the time I met Red—nearly twenty years later—she existed as a shadow: the woman arriving on the back porch at night to ask for money. I never saw her face or heard her name. One night, numbed or drugged, she fell asleep forever.

She was, perhaps, disillusioned beyond redemption—or, equally plausible, the exact opposite: an unrepentant radical unable to endure the claustrophobia of moribund times. If Red despised the Lincoln brigadiers who lived in the past, she seemed as unwilling to accommodate his shift toward piecemeal improvements. His was a Catholic temperament, dedicated in its way to a world of endless struggle, small victories, and many losses. Hers, ironically, was that of the evangelical apocalypse, not much different from those Protestant missionaries—the Dulles brothers, for example—who waged the cold war against her. She refused to make compromises. In any event, neither of them fit the stereotype of the ex-revolutionary—the old radical gone sour with age —who so often wound up supporting the other side.

Red had kept the faith, but he tempered the zeal of the Marxist dialectics with a gentle respect for the human scale. I remembered a party at his house, less than a year before, when a young Iranian student mentioned her suspicion that the shah's SAVAK would pursue her to San Francisco. "You come here," Red assured her. I recalled the spring weekend, just a few weeks earlier, when Red solved the problem of how to ship a truckload of used clothing to the refugees in Mozambique: He drove to a nearby warehouse, picked the lock, and appropriated a couple of packing crates. "He was always a revolutionary," someone had said, "always an internationalist. We were all family."

I understood now how his brothers' estimations converged: to the Jesuit priest, Red was a man of religion; to the scholar, an inspired pedagogue. For Red never attempted merely to impart information, to provide the missing facts and details of a lifetime (so that, perhaps, some ex–academic historian might produce the perfect oral history). He did not ordinarily spout wisdom. (My instincts about ignoring the tape recorder, at least in that sense, were correct.) What he did instead, through a healthy disrespect for authority and an incorrigible sense of justice, was to make a person aware of what he already knew—the logic, the morality, the necessity of choice.

If history is essentially an exchange between the past and the present, a dialogue that crosses time, whom one chooses to address (who responds to the call) is surely no accident. Red represented the best of the radical tradition—a living history of prin-

cipled dissent from a variety of orthodoxies, whether Catholic or
Communist, civilian or military. He was nonetheless (as he well
understood) an endangered species. And I was looking for a historical lineage, political and personal, seeking solid precedents
for my own antiauthoritarian tendencies. We met at the right
time. In Red I found confirmation and continuity. So, I like to
think, did he.

As I puzzled over these symbiotic relationships, Anna gave me
some audiotapes she thought might help. There were five in the
bundle. The first was my own interview with Red in his kitchen.
The second consisted of the eulogies from his memorial service.
The third tape was broken; there was no message. The fourth
contained only a brief, one-sided telephone conversation as Red
discussed money with his ex-wife. The fifth was a taped letter he
sent to some relatives only a few days after we had met at that
Lincoln Battalion reunion. "I'm somewhat angry," Red intoned,
"at some of my friends who have died for depriving me of their
company." He hesitated for a second, then added: "Doesn't make
much sense, does it?"

SIXTEEN

Historical Inventions

The urge for historical preservation took a new turn after the success of Alex Haley's *Roots* in the late 1970s. Inspired by his example, oral history clubs proliferated around the country, appealing especially to those social groups—women, minorities, gays—which, like Haley's blacks, had been excluded from the traditional chronicles of our national history. In the portable tape recorder such partisan historians discovered a technique and an opportunity to bypass the academic orthodoxies that had neglected their cultural traditions. Unlike the written language, oral history diminishes the importance of an expert intermediary, the professional historian, and reduces the process of historical inquiry to its simplest form—the acquisition of raw data. Ideally, as my experience with Red testified, oral history also possesses a deep emotional commitment that transcends differences of time and age. So when a group of old revolutionaries in Berkeley, California, founded the "Radical Elders Oral History Project," I accepted an invitation to participate in their excavations.

We would try to recover the radical heritage. Having been tutored in the harsh realities of the Great Depression and also in the communist ideology of that era, these veterans of the Old Left clung to the revolutionary faith; their God had not failed. Yet they themselves had failed completely to communicate with the young radicals of the New Left in the 1960s. To them, the very idea of a counterculture more concerned with personal liberation than the class struggle was incomprehensible. Yet as they entered their seventh, eighth, and ninth decades, the old radicals expressed a desire for continuity—not just a personal link to the future but also a sense of political relevance. They saw themselves as elder statesmen of the Left. And they professed (at least in theory) an interest in learning from the young. I would eventually find out otherwise, but the theory sounded splendid.

My first assignment was to interview one of the ailing veterans of the Abraham Lincoln Battalion, known to all by his nickname, El Magnífico. "He's in pretty bad shape," I was advised, "but he had some important experiences you should record." During the Spanish civil war, so the story went, Dolores Ibarruri, "La Pasionaria," had singled out his remarkable courage; Franco had retaliated with a million-peseta bounty on his head. What had he done? In the heat of battle he had mounted a parapet and, supplied by comrades in the trenches, had thrown dozens of hand grenades—ambidextrously—into the charging enemy. Magnífico had saved the hill. He was especially notorious because of his color: The Spanish children called him El Chocolate, but, naturally, he preferred Magnífico.

When I met him in 1978, he was living on a quiet suburban street about a day's drive from San Francisco. His frame house needed a coat of paint, as did the tilted picket fence that surrounded a weedy front lawn. It was early spring. At the aluminum screen door he extended a firm handshake and invited me in. He was sixty-six then, and fat, but it was easy to imagine an athlete's body beneath the rolling gut. He wore a bright yellow tee shirt made of netted fabric over which flapped an unbuttoned orange shirt, black-and-white-checked pants held up by red-and-black suspenders, cloth slippers, no socks. He looked like a character out of Stephen Foster. When he smiled, which was often, he revealed a pair of missing front teeth.

He led me into the small living room, indicated the couch, and then deflated himself onto his personal easy chair. It faced a floor-model color TV set that was tuned to a daytime game show, though in deference to my visit the sound had been turned off.

Above him on the wall hung two color portraits—Martin Luther
King and John Kennedy. As I set up the tape recorder, Magnífico
said something in a language I couldn't understand—a Mississippi dialect that seemed to slide around his tongue and whistle
past his gums. He pointed to two bare-bodied cherubs poised atop
a pair of whiskey decanters. I didn't want to appear unapprecia-
tive, even at nine in the morning, and so Magnífico called to his
wife to bring another glass. She was younger than he and guard-
edly friendly. Magnífico held the glass carefully, and when he
lifted the cherub's arm, the boy passed a stream of bourbon from
his penis. I later suspected that Magnífico's slurred speech had
several plausible explanations, not least of which was his diet, a
mix of instant coffee, honey, milk, and gin. I counted on the tape
recorder to compensate for my slurred hearing. As it turned out,
that was an excellent plan. No one would have believed his story.

The trouble with oral history is that it can't be communicated
in any other way. The printed word may reproduce the exact language, even allow for nuance of expression, but a written dialogue
alone denies the reality of the moment, the indecipherable re-
incarnation of the past. The word on paper turns the listener into
a spectator, establishes a voice of finality, and disrupts what is
essentially only a conversation. Ironically, this separation is sometimes just what the talker wants. I've interviewed older people
who do not *want* to recapture the past. For them, the tape recorder
serves as a shield, a way not to be honest. They may answer each
and every question, but they will make no effort to cover the ribs
of my ignorance. Magnífico, by contrast, told all and—as I would
learn to my disappointment—more.

On the first day of the interview I ran through his life quickly,
trying to sketch out a basic chronology. That alone was extraordinary by its diversity and sheer excitement. He was born on the eve
of World War I in southern Mississippi, the son of a fundamen-
talist preacher who had been educated at Booker T. Washington's
Tuskegee Institute in Alabama. Magnífico's father apparently had
a violent temper. After one beating, young Magnífico ran away
from home, hoboing all the way to Los Angeles. He was not yet
eight years old! Somehow, he found his way to the beaches and

lived off the tips and handouts of wealthy sunbathers. One woman was a photographer from San Francisco named Consuelo Kanaga, who, he said, adopted him as a houseboy, exchanging room and board for various services, including work in her darkroom. It was she who introduced him to the political Left: her friends, Lincoln Steffens and Ella Winter, and through them members of the left-wing intelligentsia. Magnífico would not be more specific.

He was also fuzzy about dates. He said he helped organize a nonsegregated streetcar workers' strike in New Orleans in the late 1920s; a little later, he participated in the bloody sharecroppers' protests in Alabama and was once run out of town by a white posse; he made public speeches on behalf of the Scottsboro Boys, who were accused of raping two white women in a Depression-era cause célèbre. During the early 1930s he attended several international meetings of left-wing artists and writers in Marseilles and Rome, among other places, but his own work had been destroyed in a fire some time after World War II. In 1934 he helped his photographer friend cover the great waterfront strike in San Francisco. Two years later, he competed in a relay race at the Workers' Olympics in Barcelona, a radical alternative to the festivities hosted in Berlin by Adolf Hitler. After the outbreak of the Spanish war, he volunteered as an ambulance driver, then as a guide to escort other volunteers over the rugged Pyrenees. Later, he made speeches in several European capitals to raise money for the Spanish Republic. Eventually, he entered the Lincoln Battalion—America's first desegregated army—and fought heroically until he was wounded in 1938.

After Spain, Magnífico joined the merchant marine as a cook —one of the few maritime trades open to blacks—and had sailed aboard the last U.S. vessel to leave Japan before Pearl Harbor. The ship was bombed in the Philippines on December 8, 1941, and had limped home via the Indian Ocean. On the way, he landed in South Africa with a terrific toothache, but was refused treatment by a white dentist. So, said Magnífico with a toothless grin, he'd knocked out the dentist's teeth!

Arriving on the East Coast, he was recruited by the United States Army for a speaking tour of the South, designed to rally black support for the war. En route, he stopped in Mississippi to visit his father—the first and last reunion since he had fled west as a boy. Then he proceeded to California, where he enlisted in the army. Because of his previous military training, said Magnífico, he was assigned to teach antichemical warfare tactics at a base in Louisiana. He was one of the few blacks to instruct white soldiers—in the South or anywhere else. One night his commanding officer ordered him to lead a contingent into a nearby town to break up a riot between black soldiers and the local segregationists. He accomplished the mission without making an arrest. The CO, surprised and then alarmed by Magnífico's influence among the black troops, arranged for his transfer to another base in Texas. There, for political reasons, said Magnífico, he was discharged from the service.

Magnífico then returned to the merchant marine, survived two sinkings in the Pacific, and supplemented his occupational excitement by serving as a courier for the Communist party. After the war, he remained active in the labor movement, opposing the expulsion of left-wing unions from the CIO in the early days of the cold war. But when the Korean War broke out in 1950, he was screened off the ships as a possible subversive. He then found work in a factory and remained there until reaching the age of mandatory retirement. To supplement his small pension, he was running a hot-lunch concession out of his kitchen.

It was obvious why they called him Magnífico. Even as he spoke, his story attracted a crowd in the living room. His wife, whom he married long after the events he was describing, seemed especially impressed by the tape recorder and its connotations of her husband's importance. So was a friendly neighbor, who interrupted the narrative to describe Magnífico's later exploits as a community organizer—he led a delegation of blacks to city hall in the 1960s to demand new sidewalks and blacktop for the muddy streets. Mrs. Magnífico disappeared into the bottom of the clothes closet and reappeared with clippings to verify the claim. Magnífico basked in their approval. Was he also aware of the impression he was making on his young son-in-law, a man of about twenty who made his living as a night watchman and who now gladly surrendered a morning's sleep to hear his wife's woozy father reminisce?

I was becoming better acquainted with his accent, but as the day passed noon other factors, should we say liquid factors, began to affect his speech. His voice became flat, the words were chopped, monosyllabic. He seemed very tired and very bored. With the recorder running, I assumed I could figure it all out later. What I heard the first time was interesting enough. There remained, however, some holes in his story—missing years, the absence of names, disconnected statements that fit neither his background nor the chronology. A second run-through would be necessary, but for now I tried to fill in the blanks, prompting his memory.

Did he know Paul Robeson? "Sure." They had met in Spain. They had shared a magazine cover. Years later, they had walked together down the Champs-Elysées. But Magnífico offered no information about the great black radical.

Hemingway had been to Spain—had he met him, too? "Oh, sure." That figured: As a black comrade, Magnífico would have been a living symbol of racial solidarity in the war against fascism, a veritable showpiece. But here, too, he volunteered no contribution to the historical record.

I tested his reliability. Another journalist in Spain was Jim Lardner, son of the writer Ring, who had been killed just a few days before the Lincoln Battalion withdrew from the war. Had Magnífico met the young Lardner? "Yes." But hadn't Magnífico himself been wounded? He didn't reply.

Had he ever encountered Josephine Baker, the black chanteuse of Paris? "Asked her for money for Spain." Did she contribute? "Yes. Said, 'I hope you get your black ass shot off.'" He giggled.

He had participated in the Workers' Olympics. Did he know Jesse Owens? They had run relays together, said Magnífico, but he refused to go back to Nazi Berlin. Back? He had been run out of Germany once before. When was that? He was vague: after 1933 when Hitler came to power, but before the Olympics.

What about the years between? In 1934 he had helped the mysterious Consuela Kanaga take photographs of the San Francisco

General Strike. He had attended those artists' conferences in Italy and southern France. He had been involved in the National Negro Congress. But whenever I tried to clarify the sequence or find out who led him where, Magnífico retreated to silence.

Was he really an artist? He had won a prize for some water-colors but said he didn't really deserve it. Anyway, the paintings had been burned. A writer? He grunted, then rose from his chair and went to the back of the house. He returned with a yellowed magazine, a publication of the WPA called *American Stuff*. Inside was a story he had written about tramping. Did that justify those international writers' meetings?

The whites of his eyes were bright red. We would have to post-pone further discussion. Besides, I already had plenty of leads that required checking, particularly his claim to have met Jim Lardner in Spain. I had already shut off the tape recorder when I noticed a big question mark in my notes. How had he become an expert in chemical warfare, sufficiently qualified to teach the subject for the U.S. Army?

"Did you learn that in Spain?" I asked casually.

He shook his head. "No. With the Red Army."

What? Where?

"In Russia."

Now I understood his reticence (I thought). Who was I to come prying into his affairs, asking sensitive questions about the past? Naturally he was suspicious. Did my color matter? Even with bona fide introductions I was a total stranger. Why should he trust me?

Here, however, were the missing years.

"How long in Russia?"

"Six months."

"Then what?"

"Went to China. Taught them that stuff."

"You taught antichemical warfare to the Chinese Communists in 1935, 1936?"

Magnífico nodded. The pieces fell slowly into place.

A writer I knew had just completed a book about the women photographers of San Francisco. She not only recognized the name Consuela Kanaga but had interviewed the old woman in upstate New York, just before her death. Had Kanaga ever mentioned her darkroom assistant? No, but she did like to photograph black people, including such activists as the poet Langston Hughes. She was certainly interested in left-wing causes. That part of Magnífico's story, so implausible on its face, had held up.

The Lardner acquaintance was another matter. If Magnífico had been shot in the leg at the time and place he said he was, it would have been impossible for him to have met the journalist. But why would he make it up? Was it mistaken identity? Had his memory failed? Did he simply not want to offend me by admitting his ignorance, in the same way that certain natives would rather misdirect a tourist than provide no information at all? Such possibilities challenged the value of the entire interview. Not to mention that he could have been lying.

I mentioned the problem to several veterans of the Lincoln Battalion who had known Magnífico. None could explain the apparent contradictions. I was advised to contact one of Magnífico's old friends, a labor union leader who still lived in the city. He had served in Spain as a political commissar, one of a group of volunteers who accompanied the soldiers in training and in battle to provide a political rationale for the war and boost morale. Some of the commissars had reputations for ideological rigidity; one black commissar, according to Magnífico, had been cashiered for cowardice. But collectively they preserved a remarkable élan among the troops, despite overwhelming physical hardships and military defeat. And some, like my contact in San Francisco, had earned a considerable reputation for bravery.

He had witnessed Magnífico's exploits in Spain—participated in a battle at one of those hills when a few hundred international brigadiers defeated thousands of fascists, thanks, in part, to Magnífico's pitching. He had also seen Magnífico shot in the leg. In fact, he was the person who had come to Magnífico's side and carried him back to safety. He had no trouble in explaining the contradiction in Magnífico's facts. What had happened, he said, was that Magnífico had mixed up the battle numbers of the hills. As a result, I had deduced the wrong dates. So Magnífico might well have met Jim Lardner in Spain, though no one could verify it. The former commissar also thought it plausible that Magnífico had met Hemingway and Robeson. About Jesse Owens he wouldn't guess. He knew nothing about the Barcelona Olympics or about Magnífico's political missions around the world.

I returned to Magnífico twice more to flesh out the details of his story, to find fresh evidence and verify its authenticity. Here I was less successful. Although Magnífico would repeat the same general outline, he could no longer recall particular places or names. Too often, I found myself supplying the missing details. I also noticed that he felt most comfortable, most enthusiastic, when describing his last crusade: the demand for sidewalks and street pavement. It was, in contrast to Spain, in contrast to the whole left-wing movement, a palpable victory. Through it all—twelve hours of questioning—his young son-in-law sat silently in the room, mystified by the old man he had known previously only as a cook and sandwich maker. When at last I was leaving, his wife asked if someday his biography would make a good TV show. I glanced at Magnífico, sitting in his stuffed chair, but already his eyes had shifted back to the silent screen.

After more fruitless fact checking, I presented the tapes to the Radical Elders, and they hired a native southerner to transcribe the narrative. He had no trouble with the text—only with its credibility. He wanted to believe it—everyone who heard it did—me most of all, for its veracity would not only justify my labor; it would vindicate my belief that history, in the last analysis, is an act of empathy, a trust between past and present.

Eventually, I located other people who knew Magnífico in his salad days. One retired journalist remembered him marching into the offices of a left-wing newspaper dressed in a nineteenth-century soldier's uniform and brandishing a sword that terrorized the women employees. "Colorful" was his conclusion. He also assured me that it was possible to verify the most intriguing aspect of the Magnífico legend: his training in the Red Army and the subsequent mission to China. On my behalf, he would contact a former Communist party official in New York who could absolutely confirm the story, one way or the other.

I was not entirely eager for the result. The situation reminded me of an earlier incident when an old friend came for a visit. We had gone to grade school together, then to college. Twenty-five years earlier, he was the person who persuaded me to join the staff of the college newspaper, my first political awakening. In those years we shared a complete intimacy, the candor of happy boys. Now he was a college professor in the South. We had not seen each other in a decade, but over a bottle of bourbon we found ourselves touching those bedrock truths that inhabit one's personality. Our common past served as a reservoir of purity—a time of total honesty that foreclosed any deceit, even those mild mythologies that people invent about themselves for no particular purpose.

In the course of this reunion my friend described a long, sordid life with drugs. He told me about marathon experiments and lucrative deals that amazed and shamed him. He told me that once, in a hotel room in Chicago, he shot a drug dealer, killed the man over a tardy payment. He described the scene in its intricate details: the face, the noise, the blood on the flowered couch, the flight down the stairs. He also told me that he had never told anyone else, not even his wife, about the murder. I felt like a priest hearing a confession. Then, after a long embrace, he went away.

The following day my friend called to thank me for my hospitality. "You remember that story I told you?" he said, knowing very well that I would. "None of it was true." I felt stunned, betrayed: angry not only that he had undermined my trust but that he had invalidated the entire reunion. Was the whole evening a lie? Was the past so plastic that its shape had no value?

I remained uneasy about Magnífico's verdict. At last it came—and in one word: "bullshit."

Voltaire said that "history is only a pack of tricks we play upon the dead." I've always suspected it was the other way around. As for Magnífico, I had to abandon his story. Most of it was certainly true; maybe even now this friend of a friend was also wrong. And if Magnífico had so little faith in history—given his experiences, who could blame him?—there was nothing more that I could do. Magnífico has been dead now for about five years. So are most of the Radical Elders, and their project as well. What was lost is not some particular truth, a rash of information, but a simple, more delicate tissue of connection. Among the Teton Sioux there is a wise, premonitory aphorism that "a people without history is like wind upon the buffalo grass." Reluctantly, I came to understand that just because someone is old does not mean he has something to say.

SEVENTEEN

Looking for an Old Flame

I n the absence of history one succumbs easily to its mutant
form—nostalgia, a malady that appears in a particularly viru-
lent form during the mid-life crisis. I had just passed forty,
found myself "between projects" with time on my hands, and all
I could do was contemplate the unexpected turnings of my career
and wonder where I was heading. But instead of looking forward,
I retreated into the past.

Some memories, I am sure, are best left undisturbed; they
refresh us at a distance. But some memories will not rest: We
scrutinize them, the way the Greeks examined the corpses of
dead birds, to see how they forecast our lives. So it was with a
woman named Sara. As I moved into my middle age, I found myself thinking about her often—no, obsessively!—and about what
might have happened had we stayed together.

The last I heard, she was living on the northern coast of California, in a small town near a river that emptied into the Pacific.
That was all I could remember. And there was something she said
in that last long-distance conversation about herbs and healing,
natural foods and childbirth. Was she still a child of the sixties?

So I telephoned a former colleague named Michael, the only
person I knew who lived in that neck of the woods, and allowed
him to invite me up for a holiday. He had his own motives. At the
age of forty-one, with patches of gray spreading through his dark,

kinky hair, he was experiencing a familiar academic crisis. He had taken a year off from teaching and was supporting himself by playing the piano in the nightclubs and bars that sprouted in the rainy climate of northern California. He had just lost thirty pounds on a crash diet: his own rendition of the mid-life crisis, I surmised. Now he was rushing to the edge of another decision. He wanted to quit his job, abandon his academic career, and become a musician. Or so he said. Anyway, it was a good excuse to go. "It will do you good," said Alice, my housemate, and she said it twice.

I left San Francisco on Saint Valentine's Day, an unseasonably glorious day, and landed an hour later in the middle of a cloudburst. As if in protest, my left foot instantly swelled up with an attack of gout, a torment that came into my life as a fortieth birthday present.

"You look great," Michael assured me as I limped toward his mustard yellow Mustang. He looked great, too: tanned; his hair full and frizzy; his body pencil thin inside a hip-length black leather coat. As the little car shrieked away from the curb, he snapped a cassette into the audio system, and the loud heavy metal racket ended any further conversation.

Michael's passion for the new music contrasted with the staid surroundings. His neighborhood reminded me of the Midwest: wide residential spaces, Victorian mansions with spiral turrets and broad porches built next door to clapboard bungalows. The lawns were neat, and the large, bare trees testified to a ripe stability. He led me past a shingled Victorian to his rented carriage house in the rear. It was cold inside and stark. The furniture was secondhand, and while everything was neatly arranged—the magazines stacked perfectly, the books even with the edges of the shelves—there was an underlying odor of dust, as if the place hadn't been cleaned properly since his second wife moved out two years ago. I settled my stuff in his study.

"Anything special you want to do?" he asked.

I mentioned Sara. She lived around there on the coast—near a river, I thought. She was into natural foods or something. Did he want some adventure?

He seemed unperturbed. "I've got something lined up for to-night," he promised. "And tomorrow night we've got tickets for a new show. That leaves Saturday. We can find her on Saturday."

It was raining hard by the time we landed at a glitzy bar called the Yellow Peril. Michael waved to the bartender, a dark-haired beauty, and led me to a corner table with an excellent vantage of the front door. The waitress took our orders and returned with a tray of drinks—and a gift box for Michael: "It's from Carla." He waved again to the woman behind the bar. We clinked glasses, and then he untied the red ribbon, tore off the wrapping, and extracted a pair of aqua bikini underpants with a red heart sewn into the crotch. He blew Carla a kiss.

The next stop was an old hotel bar where the setting was more genteel and the drinks more expensive. Michael was looking for someone, but it wasn't either of the two young couples that stopped to say hello. Both men shook hands politely and then receded, like mild waves slapping a beach. The women, how-ever, lingered. They were young: urban coeds—twenty or twenty-two years old with razor-sharp hair (one bright red, the other jet black), lipstick, rouge, eye shadow, and cigarettes. They rubbed like cats against the edge of the table, making untimid eye contact with Michael, until one of the men reminded them that it was time to go.

"I'm just a romantic," said Michael after they left. "I'm really attracted to the young ones."

"We'd make a fine foursome," I suggested, only half in jest; "two retired schoolteachers and a couple of coeds old enough to be babysitters."

"Don't complain," he said.

The Thursday night special turned out to be a New Wave musical about cocaine dealers, a subject that the audience knew something about. The singing was horrible; the acting nonexis-tent. But the theater was filled with laughter and spontaneous applause. I could see that the show formed part of Michael's dissi-dent culture, but through the performance he seemed distracted and uncomfortable. When it ended, I found out why.

She stood in the dark, smoky hallway, sultry as a kitten—

a Lauren Bacall look-alike in a black silk blouse, black leather pants, and suede boots; her light brown hair slid halfway across her forehead. The eyebrows were full; her lips moist and generous. Michael left me alone. Half an hour later, he brought her to the table.

He had known Elena for less than a week. Like the other women he attracted, she was a student—but somewhat older, say twenty-eight, and she had lived alone for several years in Morocco, which gave her a certain self-confidence and mystery. She did not chatter like the others; she seemed instead to be listening with an immense intensity to sounds I couldn't hear. Michael told her about our plans to find Sara on Saturday, and she asked to come along for the ride.

We slept the next day until noon and spent the rainy afternoon indoors. Michael looked wasted, but he kept the decibel level high. "This music is my ticket to the future," he explained, as if he had rehearsed the line. "It keeps me feeling young."

The night moved like an instant replay—from bar to theater to bar. Eventually he found her at a roadside tavern. Sitting at the bar, Elena looked even younger than she had the previous night; the stark absence of makeup accentuated her pallor. How had she survived in the macho culture of Morocco? Against the swelling electric rhythms she possessed a calm serenity, betrayed only by the slight furrow in her brow and her constant smoking.

We wound up in an all-night diner, where for the first time since sunset it was possible to hear a human voice. Hers was deep and crisp—and newly animated. She was describing North Africa, more particularly the wonder of the Arab men. Michael, feeling threatened, said something hostile about his Arab students.

"But they're so vulnerable," she said.

"They're contemptible," he replied angrily. "They're the ones who cheat. They buy term papers. They cheat on tests. I have no respect for them. I hate what they stand for."

"That's their culture. That's what they believe. That's the only way they know how to get ahead in this country."

"They're imperialists. They have no respect for our morality."

"No, you're an imperialist. You're imposing your standards."

"They have no standards."

"They can't survive any other way."

They went on this way: Michael defending an academic tradition he would reject on most other counts; Elena romantically supporting the underdog. She was, in fact, afire for the first time. Never mind, for the moment, the issues at hand or the logic of the argument. At dawn in a seedy cafe, Elena would stand up for an idea, fight with enthusiasm and honesty. She had no regard for Michael's mounting anger. Nor was she intimidated by his education. No, she denied his reality; to her—to anyone with a particle of decency, she said, banging her fist against the table— the literal survival of a poor immigrant people was more important than any academic ethics. The spectacle was worthy of the Friday night fights.

And this, I saw, was exactly what Michael desired in her—in the gathering of young, hip, half-educated women. They were the antithesis of the professional style: undisciplined, raw, willing to flirt with any fashion or neat-sounding cause, willing to appear foolish about their politics—they could even go fascist, he remarked later, with a peculiar sense of pride—as long as they could identify with an unvarnished human principle. Where Michael saw cheaters and hustlers, Elena defended necessity. He could never be so careless.

On Saturday we headed west along the Trinity River to the coast. The sun was already ahead of us, casting shadows on the rugged slopes that framed the turning river. Michael had calculated the itinerary: after we reached the ocean, we would head south, passing through such towns as Blue Lake, Arcata, and Eureka; then, if that failed, we would head inland to Fortuna, Rio Dell, and Pepperwood. There were few enough natural-food folks in the area, he assured me; someone was bound to know Sara if she were still there. The views, he promised, would be spectacular.

"I hope she's worth the trouble," Elena said with a smile. "Who is this Sara?"

"The missing link," I quipped. That was partly true. "The first step."

Twenty years ago Sara had been everything to me; in that time of arch-monogamy we had been lovers. Well, adulterers. She was blond, blue-eyed, midwestern: a farmer's daughter, tall and strong. In all those dreary years of graduate school, Sara was the one exception—the only time I broke the rules, did something I thought was wrong. But it wasn't a guilty conscience that kept her alive in my thoughts—just the opposite. Where else might she have led me?

It was hard to explain my ambivalence to Elena: the guilt, the risk. "You discover just how dishonest you can be. You discover that you can lie and be good at it. You, the one doing all these terrible things: It's still you. It can destroy your self-image."

Michael had a different experience. He admitted he'd been a virgin until the age of twenty-four. His first lover was having a simultaneous affair with one of Michael's professors. He told a story about being caught by her husband, only it seemed they *wanted* to be caught, so they could end the business cleanly. This was twenty years ago, not exactly the Middle Ages, but he also remembered the fear—and the reality—of unwanted pregnancy.

"We thought we were good people," I said to Elena, "but it was hard to be good, and once we were bad, it was hard to see what was so bad."

Did she understand? "The sexual revolution came before the other revolutions—chronologically, in our own lives. Make Love, Not War. It wasn't a bumper sticker," I said.

We entered the outskirts of a large town, drove past Sears and Wards, every food franchise ever established anywhere, down an auto row, past a run of three-bungalow motels built in the 1940s for wartime mill workers. The highway split into a one-way street that passed the downtown banks and an ancient movie palace called the Orpheum. Then, to my amazement, before us in large capital letters, NATURAL FOODS welcomed us to town.

Sara was not the woman behind the counter. Nor, while we waited for her to ring up a customer, could I find Sara's name on the hand-lettered posters for Rolfing and Lamaze classes. The store was neat and orderly: rows of hand-filled Mason jars with herbs and spices; packages of dried fruits and boxes of whole-

grain cereals; a tankard of freshly ground peanut butter, enam-
eled honey pots, and crocks of black-strap molasses—ample testimony to the toils of a prospering shopkeeper. On the walls were
photographs of women bodybuilders.

"Sexy!" said Michael.

"Young," I replied. It struck me now that Michael's obsession
with young women was a way of making up for twenty-four years
of virginity and a multitude of love affairs he hadn't had. For
all his talk about feeling young, he too seemed locked into the
past. Maybe Michael's enthusiasm for starting over again—a new
career, a new lover—meant just the opposite of what it appeared
to be: not optimism but a fear of the future, a denial of middle age.

The natural foods saleswoman was less than outgoing, but admitted she knew Sara; indeed, she worked for her. But Sara lived
forty miles away and hadn't been to the store for several days.
She wasn't sure we could find her.

"I'm an old friend," I explained, giving her my card. "In case
we miss her, would you give her that. Say hello."

Having come this far, I still might not see her. "How is she? Is
she doing all right?"

"She's expecting a baby next month."

I telephoned from a pay phone in a nearby restaurant. A child
answered. When I asked for Sara, she dropped the receiver on the
floor and yelled "Ma." But then a man picked it up: another voice
from the past. It took Sara some time to get on the line. She was
surprised, then embarrassed because her house was a wreck. Her
husband was sick; the cat had delivered kittens in the closet; one
of her goats had just pissed on the couch. "I'm a mess," she said.

"Comb your hair and meet us here," I suggested.

We drank coffee while we waited—Michael and Elena on one
side of the booth, me and the empty place on the other.

I suddenly felt uncomfortable about introducing her to them.
Would they find her attractive? Would I? She was a part of my
past, but perhaps a part best left buried in the psyche. Why had
she been so important to me then? Why now?

My anxiety was producing an acute clarity. All the glib and
funny opening lines I could imagine somehow turned in my mind

to solemn philosophical statements. This reunion, begun as a lark, had turned into a dramatic denouement. Michael and Elena had moved from the status of innocent spectators to active participants. The parallels seemed obvious: Elena and Sara, Michael and me. Wasn't it my youth I was pursuing so ardently?

Never before had I seen Sara after dark. To my relief, she looked terrific. Her hair was shorter, but it had the same healthy luster I remembered, and her perfect smile edged slightly upward at the corners. That was "our song": "Shadow of Your Smile." She gave me a hurried, nervous hug. Despite eight months' pregnancy, her body felt lean and hard beneath the green poncho she wore. And her tenseness, even that was familiar, for our relationship had always been furtive. Yet I would have walked right past her on the street.

We traded facts: her daughter was eight; my son lived with his mother. She owned the natural foods business as well as the farm nearby; I had just finished a book about fame. I had come here for a vacation; she had just returned from Texas. I told her news about old friends; she had none to tell. We were glad when Michael and Elena said they were going for a walk.

"I've known you longer than almost anyone else in my life," I said.

She nodded. "It wasn't meant to be. I'm not that person any more."

"Who is? Not me, either. But I think that's because of you."

"You were so serious. You were going to have a great career." She spoke without a trace of sarcasm. "I guess you have."

"I did. But then it came up empty. It wasn't enough. Do you still read Trotsky biographies?" I asked, turning the tables.

She laughed. Who else would know so much about her academic past?

"Before I met you," I said, "I did everything right. Maybe I would have gone on like that forever—a strip of blacktop in Kansas."

"You always hated the Midwest."

"No, really. I could have gone on forever," I repeated. "After a certain point, it was so easy."

"I know," she said.

"But then you came along. Broke the egg. I discovered there was something besides a career. Something inside I'd never noticed. At least it seems like that in retrospect."

"You know, Peter," she said. "Do you remember what the alternatives were? You wanted to get divorced from your wife and marry me." She turned to face me. "Then you didn't."

She was right. The alternatives to marriage then always seemed to be another marriage. It wasn't just social convention that pushed in that direction. It was temperament. We needed—she and I needed—a sense of structure. It was more important than our desire for ecstasy. In those days I could speak eloquently about Camus and Sartre—the existential anxiety of freedom—because for me it was true.

"I should thank you for my freedom," I said.

"Don't," she said softly. She looked at her watch. "I've really got to go. My husband is sick."

I slid out of the booth and stood next to her. Our eyes locked for a second and we kissed, and then she turned toward the door. She walked a few steps. "I should say goodbye to your friends."

We found them in the parking lot. "Nice meeting you," she said. I walked her through the dark to her van. She turned to kiss me again—just a second longer than the first time.

Now she was gone: red taillights trundling toward home.

The flame had not even flickered. Sadness was my first feeling —an uncontrollable grief. In the darkness, I hid my tears.

It took a while for me to accept what had happened. For twenty years Sara had lived in my imagination as a timeless possibility —ever the temptation to escape, be reborn. Of course I knew we were both getting older, and even, perhaps, growing in antagonistic directions. That was reasonable. But what I hadn't expected was that my fantasies would also age; I hadn't realized until then that the dreams of middle age required different—should I say mature—expressions. There was no going back.

And that was why Michael's preferences for young women seemed to me so irrelevant. No, I didn't yearn to be twenty again.

As we drove back along the twisting mountain road, I felt my body lighten, I felt released and unburdened. The Sara I had just kissed was a stranger, someone else's fantasy; and the other Sara, the one I loved, at last had vanished, probably forever, into the past. And I realized that it was one thing to live in the past; and something very different to accept the timefulness of my life and to live it with good memories.

Timekeepers

I nside the brightly lit microfilm reader it is January 1958. Outside, it is twenty-five years later and dark. The room in the library basement is kept dark so the microfilm will shine. Through the dusty lens I wind the *Montgomery Advertiser,* Alabama's capital-city newspaper, published six days a week. I'm pursuing the early career of former governor George Wallace. In 1958, long before he became a symbol of southern defiance, he was running for governor for the first time. What forgotten morsels will I discover? A photograph? A speech? An inconsistency yet unknown? My hand cranks the film through the viewer, teasing my eye with old news, old gossip. Gradually I become preoccupied with this other "news," now twenty-five years old.

It is always unexpected. Near the end of the month I spot a remarkable story from Bluff City, Tennessee. Five youngsters— David H., ten; his sister Pamela, thirteen; her best friend Dorothea M., eleven; and two others unnamed—decided to cross over the icy Holston River by way of the railroad trestle instead of the old road. But the boy and his friends became dizzy on the exposed track and had to turn back. Pamela and Dorothea were braver and went ahead, feeling the familiar vibrations beneath their feet. The freight was on time. When they heard the whistle, they started quickly for the nearby water barrel. But Pamela suddenly stopped in mid-stride, pulled by the screech of Dorothea, who had caught her foot under a tie. Pamela ran back to help, grabbed at the foot, and saw the freight lumbering forward. Again Pamela bolted for safety, but again stopped dead at the sound of Dorothea's scream. "This time," the *Montgomery Advertiser* reports, "Pamela dashed to Dorothea, took her in her arms, and the two faced the freight engine together."

In sheer terror I grind the handle of the microfilm reader. (It will be five years before I muster the courage to go back and copy the quote.) Now it is March 1958 in the *Montgomery Advertiser,* and I spot a three-frame photo sequence, shot by an amateur photographer, of a father and mother watching their daughter killed in a traffic accident. She is the same age as my own daughter, reason enough for shock, but I am glued to the page by the familiarity of the sequence, seen in so many subsequent movies of slow-motion violence—the Zapruder film of Kennedy killed in Dallas, for example, or *Bonnie and Clyde*—and I realize how the public theater of death, so common in recent years, pales before the private horror.

The real research interrupts my thoughts. This same month, March 1958, candidate George Wallace assures the students at Troy State College that the best way to prevent the desegregation of public schools in Alabama is to keep the peace. "No one is as smart as us," he says (or that, at least, is the way the *Montgomery Advertiser* reports his speech). Among the student body, Wallace wins the straw poll. He exudes confidence. Today, Wallace is the surprise come-from-behind candidate. It will be another two months before his hopes will be crushed by a more popular man. But because he doesn't know the future, as I do, Wallace happily leads the campaign into Gadsden and points north.

I decide to look only for good news. It is now April 1958, and the "news" comes from the University of Minnesota, the very campus at which I had taught for five years. As I read the story, my mind summons the red-brick architecture, built to withstand the cold, and I remember that awful gray day when I stood at the rail of the Washington Street Bridge. It is almost the same time of year. A noted botanist, Dr. Robert Withdrow, had just completed a lecture on the effects of radiation on small organisms when he collapsed on the floor. Fortunately, he was near the medical school. A team of doctors, working in a waiting room, slashed into his chest and, through massage, brought his heart back to life. According to the story, Dr. Withdrow was still in critical condition. The procedure, just a decade and a half before the introduction of bypass surgery, is considered a miracle of modern medicine. I am understandably skeptical. I decide to find out exactly when Dr. Withdrow died, just how much life he had gained. The answer, found in the *New York Times* obituaries, is startling. Dr. Withdrow did not live through the night.

What haunts me about these stories is their proximity. We assume that history is about other people. But it's only chance—a heart attack in the lecture hall, a collision on the railroad trestle —that transports their names, their faces, into the official record. There, on the pages of old newspapers, go people like us. Who cannot feel the terror of Pamela H. and Dorothea M.? Or sense the trauma brother David may still hold?

And while I am mulling over the unmiraculous death of Dr. Withdrow, I start to notice a series of odd coincidences. The *Montgomery Advertiser* reports that a child actor named Eddie Hodges is having trouble getting working papers because of the local labor laws. The same month another small-town newspaper, the Alton, Illinois, *Evening Telegraph*, prints a photograph of the same Eddie Hodges, who is appearing locally in a traveling show. A switch in my memory snaps shut. I recall from another clipping that Eddie Hodges had appeared on a TV game show called "Name that Tune," whose object was to identify songs played by the studio orchestra. The contestants wore sneakers. Upon recognizing the melody, they raced to ring a bell. Eddie Hodges had a partner on the show, a Marine aviator who had just established the coast-to-coast speed record. His name was John Glenn, Jr. After he became famous as an astronaut, Glenn often reminisced about his childhood in New Concord, Ohio, comparing his life there to a once-popular Broadway show. "You see, my hometown was a real-life version of *The Music Man*," Glenn told a reporter in 1974. I look again at the caption beneath Eddie Hodges's picture in the Alton *Telegraph*. The name of his new show is *The Music Man*.

It is more than coincidence, I believe, these interlocking grids.

We humans are creatures of relationships—always seeking, building, reconstituting connections outside ourselves. Usually they are personal, the stuff of family and friendship, the unobserved love, say, between Pamela H. and Dorothea M. Some relations are remote and symbolic, the links between politicians (like Wallace) and their constituents, celebrities (like Eddie Hodges) and their fans. Some are made of pure imagination, fleeting memories merged with fantasy; we identify with the objects of our desire. Together these attachments form a living tapestry, a community in time.

The threads of history, taut and delicate as the balance of nature, knit us all. We inhabit the ecological whole. It is a moment of time no less than a position, a place, a residence. Ecology, from the Greek root *oikos*, meaning "home," possesses a chronological dimension: yesterday, today, tomorrow, the then and the now, all interwoven inseparably. We ourselves dwell inside the web, live on its strands, in the same way the Earth speeds within the Milky Way. Memory and history help us locate our connections. For we are all from somewhere else, heirs and descendants; one day soon we shall all become precedents and antecedents.

As I read the old newspapers I see the connections to my own life. I want so much to report the "news" to my father, especially that double-edged story about Dr. Withdrow. I'm sure he read it himself. In 1958 my father was forty-three, the same age I am today, and to all appearances in the prime of his life, though already he had begun an imperceptible descent. In January that year, the last month of life for Pamela H. and Dorothea M., my father's brother (my uncle Al) died of a heart attack at the age of forty-nine in his home in Connecticut. He had been a saxophone player, short-order cook, better-than-average gambler. Once, in a crap game in a roadside tavern near Hartford, he won—and collected —valuable lakefront property, along with a country house with a huge fireplace and rooms full of furniture. This improbable turn of fortune disturbed my father, undermining some primal sense of fair play among siblings. They quarreled easily and often, in the symbiotic way that only intimate relatives can fight. Al's death prevented any belated reconciliation. My father's obituary, spoken impulsively to my mother (not intended for my ears): "What a wasted life!"

This death, the first I experienced personally, accelerated my adulthood, but for my father it signaled a different turn. He had lived close to sudden death since his own teenage years in New York, when, in three weeks' time, both of his parents died of heart attacks. They were forty-nine, just like my uncle Al. My father understood the arithmetic. Never too careful about his health, a heavy smoker and eater, he figured he had five, maybe six years left.

His fatalism was qualified. He turned ferociously to a crash diet he had found: eggs. He would eat nothing but eggs, breakfast, lunch, and dinner, as many as he wanted, cooked in any way and as often as he cared. Given the calories and the cholesterol, one assumes the diet worked on the principle of eventual repulsion and disgust. If so, it failed to reckon with his appetite. As for smoking, he quit cold turkey—for a day. But he continued to shop around for a better therapy until he found a sympathetic doctor who assured him that smoking was not so bad.

He abandoned austerity, instead seizing a remedy that satisfied his curiosity: psychoanalysis. Therein he hoped to eliminate his fixations on food and tobacco. For years my father commuted to the shrink. Freud entered his daily discourses and, consequently, mine, too. He delighted in making odd extrapolations of other people's dreams, which taught me very quickly how to repress them. What he said about me to his therapist I have no idea. Once, he invited me to accompany him. When I asked him how these matters worked, he said that the doctor usually started with simple questions. "Such as what?" I inquired. "Oh," he said, "your name, your religion, what you thought about the last time you masturbated." That was as close as I ever got to the couch.

He would return from these sessions buoyant, full of life, his arms loaded with kogelhopf and strudels he had bought at the German bakeries on the upper East Side where refugee psychoanalysts abounded. On these joyous homecomings I would ask for my allowance. These were times for breaking bad news, showing report cards, explaining why I had not been accepted into the local college. Later, when the college exhausted the waiting list and reversed the decision, he gave me a ten-dollar bill. So for him psychoanalysis did work: He continued to eat too much and to smoke, but he became mellower, at least on the edges.

As he had predicted, his heart attack came when he was forty-nine. It did not kill him. He recovered, in the physical sense, and he resumed his habits with a familiar indifference to the consequences. But now he carried around himself the aura and the awe of a survivor. He had lived longer than any other member of his family, as far as he knew, and he really couldn't believe that he was alive. That made him more eager than ever to prove his own reality.

It was then that he discovered the clocks. My father, until then a musician and a schoolteacher, decided to become a clockmaker. He printed business cards, naming himself The Old Timer, and he filled the walls of our house in Queens with ticking anachronisms. Some showed tooting birds or ruddy-faced peasants parading across the face; one resembled a coloratura about to burst her seams. These clocks had personalities. My father would set each one at a slightly different time, the better to enjoy their individuality. We became adept at distinguishing the quarter hour from the half, though no one ever knew the time of day.

His interest in clocks coincided, curiously, with my own discovery of time. He had gone out one weekday afternoon to visit my sister in Manhattan and had stumbled into one of those schlock shops that proliferate on upper Broadway. He had intended to buy a rocking chair he'd seen in the doorway, but the proprietor refused to sell it. The man was more than willing, however, to part with an old maple-wood wall clock that did not work. The lines were straight; the case formed a rectangle and curved into a dome on the top. The original glass was there, and across it in gold letters was the word REGULATOR. My father saw through the dust, and he paid in cash.

I remember the incident so clearly because it happened on the same day I received a letter of acceptance to study history in graduate school. I had my own sense of time. I was twenty and in a great rush to get on with the work of my life. I had decided to become a historian: I wanted to find things at their beginnings. I was fascinated by the earliest American history, the contact between Europe and America, probably because it had nothing to do with my own history and because my ancestors were considered foreigners here unto my own generation. I believed then that history should be objective, impersonal. But there was no small arrogance in my heart. History, for me, was power: I wanted the power to make all those forgotten people be remembered, come alive.

On that day too, along with my letter of acceptance, came word of a scholarship. It was the first time I was offered money to do what I wanted to do. I could pursue my academic interests and have income enough to get married. I told my father the news as I helped him carry the REGULATOR into the basement.

Through that spring I made plans: summer job, reading programs, the wedding. I bought a tweedy suit to appear academic. With my fiancée I saw arty movies on the East Side, drank espresso in the Village, and secretly made love when her parents went to New Jersey for the weekend. We felt ourselves living on the edges of time, waiting to leap. By September I walked through my house like a stranger, self-conscious of every doorknob I was touching for the last time.

The REGULATOR, meanwhile, rested in the basement across two steel sawhorses. It was perfect, my father explained; all it needed to run was a pendulum. He decided to build one himself. The formula for a pendulum is the ratio of length to weight. My father could easily have ascertained the correct number by locating a similar clock. The REGULATOR, he would later admit, could be found in any secondhand shop in New York City. But he too was seeking a kind of omnipotence, some control over time. He made his own calculations. I remember him rummaging through the racks of half-filled baby-food jars for the proper size screws and nuts, which he used to fill a crude mold. He manufactured a staff from leftover pipe. He invited me down to the basement the night he bolted a big screw into the wall and positioned the REGULATOR on an even keel. Here was where I came in: "Find out the time, will you."

He adjusted the hands, closed the glass door, checked the levels, and released the pendulum. The concoction of old screws and pipe looked ridiculous, but the damn thing worked. We toasted each other with cans of diet soda and waited for the clock to stop. Tick. Tock. Tick. Tock. He put his arm around my shoulder, pulling me against his corpulent belly. "We'll just pick up a fancy brass front for it, clean up the wood, and that'll be your wedding present."

I retaliated with my own notion of time. I had recently written a paper on the Regulator Wars of North Carolina, a type of regulator about which my father knew nothing. I thought the story would appeal to his class consciousness. Besides, it gave me an occasion to prove my own merit as a timekeeper. I explained (with an undergraduate's zeal for detail) that before the Revolutionary War, the farmers of the Carolina backcountry had organized an armed rebellion, known as the Regulator Wars, to protest high taxes. Eventually, the militia put them down—which was why, I explained, the Regulators fought for the king during the Revolution. When I finished my little exegesis, my father said he had always wanted to study history but had to earn a living instead. It was, I think, his way of giving me his blessing.

That autumn, my bride and I departed for the Midwest. I had never been west of the Hudson, and the 1956 Pontiac—something I had "inherited"—drove like a Conestoga wagon. We were lost in the sensuality of our days—not in lovemaking, to be sure, but in the pleasures of opportunity. We were leaving behind the weight of family, or so we thought; leaving behind the provinciality of the East and a memory of immigrant childhoods and depression marriages that had gripped our parents and made them what we did not wish to become. It was ironic that my quest for a different future began in the past. Not my past, as I said, but in the past of someone else's Founding Fathers. There, I hoped to find my way out. To my surprise I did rather well that first term, thrived, in fact, in the academic environment. I was beginning to become a real historian.

So was my father. When I returned to New York for the Christmas holidays, he led me into the living room to show off his newest acquisition—a wooden-works clock built in Connecticut in the early 1800s. The pendulum danced behind a pastoral scene painted on the glass. He showed me where the picture had been partially scraped off by a previous owner, who was more delighted by the works inside. Here, my father said, was one of the earliest forms of mass production in the United States. Unlike the rest of his stuff, this was a veritable antique. "I fixed it, too," he said with a boyish grin. Then he opened the case and showed me some writing: "R. J. McBride, 1857." "It's older than that," he said. Then he winked and pointed to another inscription: his own initials, "L. S. C." and the date, "1964."

My father, at last, had found his calling.

A quarter of a century later, I surface from the archives of the *Montgomery Advertiser*. I want to go down to the basement again, hear the beat of the clocks. I want to drink a can of diet soda. I want to tell the story of Pamela H. and Dorothea M., recount the short resurrection of Dr. Withdrow. My father would understand my curiosity, my passion.

But again history has intervened. It is too late. The house has been sold. The clocks have been sold. What remains is a deep scar in the plaster of the bedroom wall where one of his antiques scraped away the paint as it, and he, fell to the floor. He was sixty-one when he died.

There are no old clocks in my house in California. The rare watches he gave me to celebrate special occasions—graduation, quitting my job—rest noiselessly in a safe-deposit box in a bank. I have even pulled the cord from the electric clock that hummed on my desk. I do not need to be reminded.

My father's hobby is now my own—timekeeping. And my quest is the same, too: Control is what I'm after—not to stop or even slow the gears of change but to understand the mechanism. There

are dozens of half-filled baby-food jars lined up in my head: anecdotes and reminiscences, dates and facts, coincidences and cross-
references, even discards and irrelevancies, because I believe
everything has its place. We all know that history is about time
—sequence and chronology, beginnings and endings. But history
is also about place—environment, setting, context. Where something happens is usually more important than when. Who notices
the occurrence? Whose perspective is recorded and reported?
Whose is ignored? Who lives to tell the tale?

I used to think that history was about the past: what happened
and why. It seemed sufficient to describe the Green Mountain
Boys and Philip Skene, or Samuel Johnson and the Puritans, or,
closer to the bone, Pamela H. and Dorothea M. What was past had
passed. History and today were antithetical terms; contemporary
history was an oxymoron. One looked back through a rearview
mirror. As one aged, so did the times. The more one knew, the
more one forgot. Eventually, biology supplanted history. Memory eroded, the body failed, then death, and a new generation
continued.

But history, unlike biology, is no longer natural, if it ever was.
It does not deal with infinite cycles of time, one generation rising,
flourishing, and giving way to the next. Instead, history concen-
trates on unique events and the particulars of human existence.
Its subject is not Birth, but Gwendolyn's child; not Death, but
two girls huddled on a railroad trestle. And because history is
not natural but the result of human selection, it is not neutral,
either. It is not a fleck of light striking the photographic film, but
the camera's eye focusing the lens. History, like photography, en-
deavors to freeze time in a frame. As I tell about Pamela H. and
Dorothea M., other figures, such as Governor Wallace, slip beyond the depth of field and seem to disappear. Only usually it is
the other way around, the Wallaces overshadow the multitudes.

I can see my father's lifetime in such photographs—from baby
pictures on a bear rug and days in a Boy Scout uniform through
years of baldness and diminishing strength. My memory fleshes
out the portraits. But above all he belonged to the mid-twentieth
century; he reflected its values, grappled with its contradictions,

and sought through music and clocks a sense of coherence and order. His was a normal life struggling against the inevitable equilibrium. I could mention exceptional moments—a song he composed, a clock he saved, a career he inspired—but that is not the point. For we are all exceptions to the rule. It is what makes us human, the subject of history. It is why I speak for the otherwise voiceless and the invisible.

NINETEEN

Consider the Alternatives

W hat's so great about the sixties?" asks Matthew, my eighteen-year-old son, who has just finished reading his father's prose.

"Did the world begin in 1969?" I reply.

He was still in his mother's womb when I first stood in front of a classroom and tried to make sense of American history. He was one when Nixon invaded Cambodia, three when Watergate happened, six when Saigon became Ho Chi Minh City. He has heard about these things; how can he understand them? The greatest history teachers today, alas, are television and the movies. What do they inform his generation?

Those who believe that the 1960s were a unique time may be pleased by the immense coverage now given to the Vietnam War. On the serious side, journalists have at last discovered the problems of the Vietnam veterans—the notorious "postwar syndrome," the legacy of Agent Orange, the prevailing sense of "waste." Meanwhile, movies like *Rambo* and *Platoon*—to take examples from opposite sides of the political spectrum—offer revisionist alternatives to the real war. If you didn't like the first ending, try another! Such programs, however poor as history, at least address the problem. The Vietnam War is again the subject of discussion. Well and good.

But isn't it significant that this interest in Vietnam comes at a time when the nation's leaders have embarked on another undeclared war? Why do we now hear so much about the agony of the Vietnam War and so little about Nicaragua? It's like the famous West Point aphorism: Young officers study to fight the last war. In this age of home video and push-button rewinds, we all risk the confusion between instant replay and live action. The danger no longer is that history will repeat itself; it's the likelihood that it already has.

It was the Lincoln Battalion that activated my conscience. Red's pal Jonesy phoned one day to invite me to a meeting of the veterans. I hadn't seen him since Red's funeral, but he looked about the same: thick white hair, tanned, rail thin. As he drove through the hilly suburbs across the bay from San Francisco, we recalled anecdotes of Red and chortled at his resourcefulness. Jonesy parked in front of a small house set high on the hills and turned abruptly to face me. In the sunlight his eyes flashed like blue jewels. "We're a little worried about losing all this stuff," he said earnestly. "I hope you'll agree to what they say."

A dozen people crowded into the small living room, about half of them gray heads, the rest in their twenties. I stood at the midpoint, old enough to know only some things. The older men poured red wine, passed potato chips, and tried to make us comfortable, but I was struck more by the silence that arose between self-conscious conversations. I had never seen them so quiet or so careful.

"Look," announced our gray-mustached host when it was time to get to business; "what's the use of beating around the bush? We've all been to too many funerals. We're getting to be like buffaloes and passenger pigeons. We're disappearing."

"Not yet," another vet called out. "I'm still around; I'm not leaving." Everyone laughed. "Not yet," he repeated.

"With all due respect," continued our host, nodding in the direction of the quibbler. "There's a lot of good work we can still do, should do. I'm sure we'll all go down fighting. Anyway, I will." He hesitated now, as if fighting against what he had decided to say. "It's just that we could use some help. Together we can do great things."

He laid out three conditions for membership in the veterans' organization: First, continue the tradition of the Lincoln Battalion, opposing fascism in Spain—and anywhere else in the world; second, protect the historical record and pass on the traditions of antifascism; third, consider the welfare of the veterans themselves.

It was my pride as a historian that swept me away. Of course, my political beliefs were assuredly antifascist; I'd already honored the reputation of the Lincoln Battalion. Of course I had not forgotten my experience with Magnífico. I would have to be careful. But what appealed to me now was the proximity, the accessibility, of a rare historical archive—the life stories of these veterans—and a mission to preserve it for the future. So it seemed a privilege to agree.

Participation in the Lincoln Battalion, however, was never honorary. It demanded a continuing involvement with political work, most of it, frankly, thankless. Sometimes the activity proved its own reward. For our first project we launched a national crusade to raise money to send medical supplies to Nicaragua. Back in the thirties, the Friends of the Abraham Lincoln Battalion (my parents among them) had undertaken fund-raising campaigns for ambulances. Each bore the insignia of its sponsors. I'd seen photographs of Hollywood ambulances (inscribed by such leftish luminaries as Frederic March and Gale Sondergaard), Harvard ambulances, labor union ambulances, and church ambulances. Now the recipients were giving back. We organized Lincoln Battalion ambulances for Nicaragua, and I gladly squandered my best writing on press releases for the cause. There was an undeniable satisfaction in shipping the ten blue ambulances—each with the words "SOLIDARIOS CON NICARAGUA"—and staging a bon voyage rally on the San Francisco waterfront.

"To that old man in Washington who says 'I am a contra,'" exclaimed Milton Wolff, the last commander of the Lincoln Battalion, "I say, 'I'm a Sandinista.'"

So we had reclaimed the past. We were showing that these times, the Reagan eighties, formed part of the historical process, could be understood and lived only as a function of passing time. And in my small way I shared the historical moment, and not just as a scholarly spectator. I was no longer relying on the assistance—or the barrier—of my tape recorder. I had discarded any pretense of the neutral, objective observer. But was I giving away too much?

I had not anticipated the ensuing crisis. Working so closely with these old revolutionaries—arguing about tactics, learning their stories, repeating gossip and rumor; in short, absorbing the realities of small-group nitty-gritty—all this involvement deepened my own political commitment. As I came to know them intimately and honestly, warts and all, I began to assume a personal responsibility to perpetuate this tradition. But the point was not just to keep the past alive. There are abundant newsreels and videotapes for that. Instead, I felt a desire, an obligation almost, to take some bold political action as well.

"Like what?" Alice asked sympathetically.

"You can't very well go off and fight with the Sandinistas," said Matthew, ever the realist. "You don't even speak Spanish."

Nor did I wish to risk life and limb. I saw no romance in dying in a foreign country, in dying at all. Indeed, that appeared as the great and obvious lesson of the Spanish civil war. All that horrible tragedy—the stuff of poetry and tribute, human defiance, noble sacrifice—could not match the power of the totalitarian juggernaut. As the English volunteer Esmond Romilly wrote in 1937 about the slaughter of his friends on the Madrid front, "There is something frightening, something shocking, about the way the world does not stop because these men are dead."

And yet the issue would not subside. Thinking historically, I sensed the country had reached a time equivalent, say, to 1962 or 1963, when the Vietnam War had begun and no one chose to admit it, least of all its perpetrators. Yes, Reagan had his critics. The Left found loopholes in the presidential embargo and sent medicine and material aid to Nicaragua. Christian humanitarians journeyed there regularly and returned as "witnesses for peace."

Within Congress the Democrats spoke eloquently against aiding the contra rebels; Speaker Tip O'Neill warned that the Congress soon would face another Tonkin Gulf resolution. And always, in the end, the opposition collapsed and the juggernaut rolled on.

What could a historian do?

Amid such consternation, Alvah Bessie, my first friend among the Lincolns, died at the age of eighty-one. During his long ostracism and exile, he had developed a habit of writing postcards to critics and friends alike, and in that three-by-five format he perfected the art of bestowing unsolicited advice. He never forgot an insult or an act of loyalty, and he became to dozens of unwitting recipients a friendly nag. "Keep warm and dry," he reminded me a few months before his death. "Worse weather is coming, both meteorological and political."

His career now looked like a lesson for my own. Bessie, the son of a well-heeled stockbroker, had rejected the world of business soon after college to become a writer. He showed considerable talent. During the depression he successfully integrated his art with a growing social conscience. His stories won prizes. He became a respected theater critic and book reviewer. Then, while working on the *Brooklyn Eagle,* he interviewed the novelist Andre Malreaux about the Spanish civil war and decided to go there himself. And Spain changed him forever. The death of friends and comrades provoked an unassuagable grief—call it survivor guilt—and he could never again accommodate the compromises necessary to pursue a normal career. He would not betray the dead; he would not testify before HUAC. Nor would he be quiet and let things pass. The ordeal of prison and the blacklist could never absorb the mourning inside. He became the needle through which the dead stabbed at the living world. He would not bend, and he would not break.

Bessie thus achieved an unusual coherence between his political instincts and his professional work; but at what cost? How much talent he wasted in diatribes and pleas for recompense! How much effort he gave because he thought a cause was right! How much clarity he traded—how much critical judgment he suppressed—because of prior political loyalties! And yet Bessie never deceived himself. Always he knew the price paid, the price taken away. He tallied the discounts and so raged to his dying day at all the losses he had to bear. That was the cost of his historical conscience.

Didn't he regret, I would ask him, the irreplaceable loss of his art?

What, he always wanted to know, was the alternative?

Now I raise the question again. Take away history—and consider the alternatives:

1. Bill Moyers, the broadcast journalist, asks a student when the Selma march took place; "I believe it was in the Peloponnesian War, wasn't it?"

Anyone who has taught a history course can match that: "The Tariff of Abominations raised the price of abominations, causing the south to hate the north"; "Andrew Jackson had great willpower, which is how he got nicknamed 'Stonewall' Jackson"; "the McNary Haugen farm bill established whorehouses for the farmers to deposit their excesses in"; "the United States bombed Hiroshima to celebrate the end of World War II."

"Who," an earnest black student recently wanted to know, "was Malcolm the Tenth?"

2. The flip side of ignorance is irrelevance. We have become a nation of trivia experts: state capitals, batting averages, the Academy Awards, Civil War battles and battlefields, TV reruns and quiz-show hosts, the height of our presidents, ad nauseum.

Each fact exists as a discrete entity; there is no context, no larger picture that descrambles the dots. History, in this light, resembles the evening news: a downtown fire, chemical spills on the interstate, falling interest rates, a riot in South Korea, and the local basketball team loses a game. Is the news too fragmented? Do we lack perspective? No matter: Tomorrow it will be history.

3. FDR once remarked that people who fondly remember the good old days usually have bad memories. In the absence of history, bad memories abound, though for courtesy's sake such substitutions pass for "nostalgia." (The word *nostalgia*, incidentally, has an interesting history; it means "homesickness" and origi-

nally was used to describe the sadness of travelers.) By evoking
a remote and misty past, nostalgia conjures up a time of innocence, childhood and youth, when decisions of any kind seemed
far away. No wonder, then, that nostalgia seems so appealing.
Remembering becomes a form of escape; nostalgia becomes amnesia.

Nostalgia too is usually commercial, an industry. It acceler-
ates the consumption of products and services. In fashion, for
example, it is commonplace to re-create a lost style: wide lapels,
padded shoulders, or James Dean haircuts. The oldies but goodies
can be reissued on eight-track stereo and again on CDs, while
Hollywood makes remakes and sets the dramatic action the day
before yesterday.

Such retrospection appears historical, but it has nothing to do
with history. It appeals instead to our *desire* for history. Thus a
TV commercial depicts a Sunday baseball game set in the 1890s,
creating a warm feeling for a simpler rural society, then instructs
the modern audience to go out and buy a contemporary brand of
beer or lemonade. In this way the sense of history is replaced with
a feeling of timelessness, making the product appear universal
and "natural." The connection to the past is blatantly arbitrary
and exploitative. Nostalgia is the lie in the void.

4. In Miami, Florida, in the year of the Bicentennial, a group
of protesters is threatened with arrest for distributing an in-
cendiary document, which, upon closer examination, turns out
to be the Declaration of Independence. What does it mean that
a majority of American teenagers do not understand the Constitution and the Bill of Rights? "If an educated electorate is the
best defense against arbitrary government," concludes Christopher Lasch, "the survival of political freedom appears uncertain
at best." What does it mean when a majority of citizens thinks
the Vietnam War was a "mistake" rather than the result of a particular foreign policy? What does it mean when a majority now
believes that President Nixon deserved a pardon?

5. To control history is to wield power—and vice versa.

Item: American national holidays (formerly "holy days") arrive
on Mondays, ensuring three-day weekends.

Item: On July 4, 1971, President Nixon announces that the Bicentennial of the American Revolution, planned to commemorate the Revolutionary War (1776–83), will culminate on July 4, 1976, coinciding (he thinks) with the last months of his administration.

Item: Jimmy Carter claims to be the first southern president since Zachary Taylor, conveniently forgetting Lyndon Johnson (a westerner?) and Woodrow Wilson.

Item: President Reagan, explaining that members of the Nazi SS were as much victims of World War II as the Jews they slaughtered, lays a wreath at a cemetery in Bitburg in 1985.

Call them "misstatements" (as in "the president misspoke himself"), inadvertant errors, sheer ignorance, or old-fashioned lies. As a nation, we have come to accept—if not actually expect—such authoritative deceptions. But what difference does it make?

Returning from Germany in 1985, President Reagan stopped in Spain to muster support from this newest NATO ally. He too remembered the Spanish civil war. Indeed, in Madrid the president cited the precedent of the Abraham Lincoln Battalion to justify the allocation of military aid to the contras in Nicaragua. It was, he said most earnestly, "a well-established tradition." The Lincolns, of course, fought against General Franco and his benefactors, Hitler and Mussolini. But to the amazement and horror of his hosts, Reagan stated that the battalion had fought on "the wrong side." Later, at numerous Washington press conferences, the president repeated this peculiar verdict of history.

What difference does it make? Consider the testimony of a single victim.

Walter Benjamin, a German Jewish Marxist, emerged during the 1920s and 1930s as an astute critic of twentieth-century civilization. Intrigued and also troubled by the growth of mass, impersonal societies, he endeavored to salvage the gentler values of his childhood in Berlin around 1900. "Every image of the past that is not recognized by the present as one of its concerns," he lamented, "threatens to disappear irretrievably." His essays on the history of art warned of the loss of a unique aesthetic in an age of cheap mass-produced reproductions. His explorations of urban landscapes, including ramblings through the Paris of Baudelaire, captured the simplicity of everyday life. Benjamin was an avid collector of odd facts and old books, as if such singular possessions could sustain the life of the rapidly receding past.

Then the Nazis came to power. Many of Benjamin's colleagues at the innovative Frankfurt Institute for Social Research perceived the danger and sought exile in Switzerland, Britain, eventually in the United States. Recently, I asked one of Benjamin's former colleagues to describe the critic's appearance. He referred me to the character of Aschenbach, played by Dirk Bogarde in the film *Death in Venice*—a middle-aged man with rimless eyeglasses, a full black mustache, and an agonizing sense of doom. It was a deliberate comparison. For unlike his Frankfurt colleagues, Benjamin did not wish to abandon his home and memories. He stayed on in Germany until it was almost too late. He fled at last to France, carrying a large library and a black suitcase filled with unpublished manuscripts. But the Nazis overran Paris in June 1940, forcing Benjamin to seek a precarious refuge in Marseilles. Despite failing health, a severe heart condition that robbed him of breath, he clung to that black suitcase. But the Nazis pursued him. In September 1940, almost miraculously, Benjamin obtained a transit visa, which permitted him to travel through Spain to Portugal—and thence, presumably, to a haven in America.

With a small group of friends and strangers, seven in all, Benjamin found a guide to lead the way into Spain. They went on foot, the scholar straining under the load of his black suitcase, dreading a heart attack, dreading more the loss of his life's work to the Gestapo. Up they ascended, through dewy, red-soiled vineyards, desperate, knowing only that failure meant a concentration camp and a certain death. There could be no return. The sight of Port Bou on the Spanish side brought immeasurable joy. Without delay the party of exiles went directly to the police headquarters to obtain the official entry stamps necessary to proceed. Their travel papers appeared in perfect order. It was September 26, 1940, just a year and a half after Franco's victory in the Spanish civil war.

The chief of police greeted them with new information. According to his latest instructions from Madrid, he could not permit "stateless" people to enter Spanish territory. They would have to return to France. If they refused, he would order them to a concentration camp at Figueras, where they would be transferred to German authorities. For three hours the exhausted exiles pleaded for mercy. Finally the chief relented, permitting them to spend the night in a hotel in Port Bou. The next day, however, they would have to return under police escort to France. But in the morning Benjamin summoned a friend to his room. He told her that at ten o'clock the previous night he had taken a massive dose of morphine. He refused medical treatment. Then, after giving her two letters of farewell, he lost consciousness and died.

Walter Benjamin's grave is unmarked; his precious papers, for which he had risked his life, were never recovered. His final anguish testified to the power of history, the difference between the ideals of the Lincoln Battalion and "the wrong side." Tragically, Benjamin himself had foreseen the result. "Only that historian will have the gift of fanning the spark of hope in the past," he wrote, "who is firmly convinced that *even the dead* will not be safe from the enemy if he wins. And this enemy has not ceased to be victorious."

The question, then, is not whether one lives in history, but rather in whose history one lives. Can there be an alternative? Can we ever let "the wrong side" seize the past and so control the meaning of the present and the future, too? As Voltaire said, "We owe respect to the living; to the dead we owe only truth."

Peter N. Carroll is the author of a number of books, among them *It Seemed Like Nothing Happened: America in the 1970s* and *The Free and the Unfree* (with David Noble). He lectures in history at Stanford University and in creative writing at the University of San Francisco. He also hosts "Booktalk" on KPFA-FM in Berkeley, California.